"Chris Jacobs is complete̶l̶y̶ ̶u̶n̶i̶q̶u̶e—a Washington conservative who actually cares about heath care and understands how it works, and does not work."

—BOBBY JINDAL, FORMER LOUISIANA GOVERNOR

"Chris Jacobs is one of the sharpest healthcare experts in the conservative movement. His is an essential voice in this debate about the future of our healthcare system and our freedom."

—MIKE LEE, SENATOR

"Chris Jacobs does a great job of breaking down complex policies into plain language accessible to all Americans. This book will allow doctors and patients to understand the details behind the radical Left's health care takeover."

—NEWT GINGRICH, FORMER HOUSE SPEAKER

"Chris Jacobs is indisputably one of the sharpest minds in health care reform today. His book is a tour de force for anyone seeking the intellectual ammunition to explain why a single-payer health care system is doomed to fail—and what reforms can make American health care the greatest in the world."

—JIM DEMINT, FORMER SENATOR

For inquiries about volume orders, please contact:
Republic Book Publishers
501 Slaters Lane #206
Alexandria VA 22314
editor@republicbookpublishers.com

Published in the United States by Republic Book Publishers

Distributed by Independent Publishers Group
www.ipgbook.com

Paperback: 9781645720027
Ebook: 9781645720034

Printed in the United States of America

Book designed by Mark Karis

THE CASE
against
SINGLE
PAYER

How "Medicare for All" Will Wreck America's
Health Care System—And Its Economy

CHRIS JACOBS

REPUBLIC
BOOK PUBLISHERS

contents

acknowledgments

The old hymn teaches that the gifts to the Lord most pleasing are humble, thankful hearts. Writing one's first book stands as an inherently humbling experience; it also gave me more reasons to give thanks.

At Republic Books, Al Regnery and Eric Kampmann decided to take a chance on an author, and a concept, not previously seen in book form—a leap of faith by any stretch. And the aptly named Joy Pullmann, my editor at the *Federalist*, burnished my writing and provided insightful suggestions with her usual good humor and aplomb.

I would find it difficult to list individually all the acts of kindness I have received over the years from my mother, family, friends, and colleagues. Thankfully, the unveiling of this volume will give me numerous opportunities to express my gratitude to them in person; I can't wait to do just that.

Two groups worth recognizing I cannot thank in person. First, my producer, Jen Sawyer, and the unsung staffers—Taylor Carey, Trisha Miller, and so many more—who decided to cast me on *Who Wants to Be a Millionaire?* It may seem odd to acknowledge production staff I have not seen since I walked off the show's New York soundstage more than six years ago. But the winnings from that day gave me the financial freedom to establish my own business in 2016. Without it, this book might never have existed. I won't soon forget the way their faith in me quite literally changed my life—and yes, that's my final answer.

Likewise, the faculty and staff of Allentown Central Catholic High School made an invaluable contribution to this book. Twelve years of Catholic education taught me many things. In particular, it taught me how to write. Writing a book in six weeks seems ambitious or foolhardy (or more likely, both). Either way, I could not have done it without the skills I began developing more than two decades ago and have worked to hone since. My teachers and mentors may not agree with all the ideas expressed in these pages, but I hope the skill and care with which I crafted them can do them proud.

As always, any errors or omissions are mine and mine alone.

C. S. J.
WASHINGTON, DC
MAY 4, 2019

SINGLE-PAYER HEALTH CARE BY THE NUMBERS

71%—Number of Americans who would pay *more* under single-payer health care, according to an analysis of Sen. Bernie Sanders's 2016 campaign plan by Emory University professor Kenneth Thorpe.

11,600,000—Americans enrolled in Indian Health Service (2.3 million) and Veterans Affairs (9.3 million) coverage who could actually keep their health arrangements. Approximately 300 million more Americans would lose their existing coverage.

1,500,000—Job losses hospitals could have to implement due to payment reductions included in a single-payer system, according to a study in the *Journal of the American Medical Association*. Layoffs by physician groups and other sectors of the health care system could add to this total.

2005—The year Canada's Supreme Court held that Quebec's prohibition on private health insurance—a provision included in the House and Senate single-payer bills—"interferes with life and security of the person," because "access to a waiting list is not access to care."

$17,000—Estimated annual reduction in household income after taxes and health spending under single payer, according to the White House Council of Economic Advisers. Their model demonstrates how single payer will permanently shrink.

$84,700,000,000—Total amount of fraud and improper payments in the *existing* Medicare and Medicaid programs. Expanding government-run health care to all Americans would massively increase the amount of potential waste, fraud, and abuse.

119,100,000—Number of Americans who would lose their existing coverage under the "moderate" plan to introduce a government-run "public option," according to a 2009 study by non-partisan actuaries at the Lewin Group.

1976—Year Congress first imposed restrictions on tax-payer funding of abortion. The single-payer bills would eliminate this restriction that has held bipartisan support for more than four decades, allowing for taxpayer-funded abortion-on-demand.

1,082,541—Number of Canadian patients waiting an average of five months for health care treatment, according to the Fraser Institute; the number totals nearly 3% of Canada's entire population.

$32,000,000,000,000,000—Minimum cost of single-payer legislation over ten years, according to separate estimates by both the liberal Urban Institute and conservative Mercatus Center.

A READING GUIDE TO S. 1129, THE MEDICARE FOR ALL ACT

PAGE 4—Section 102(a) makes "every individual who is a resident of the United States" eligible for the new program, encouraging foreign citizens to travel to America to receive "free" health care.

PAGE 5—Section 104(a) prohibits providers that partici-pate in the new program from "den[ying] the benefits of the program" to individuals based on a series of conditions, including "termination of pregnancy"—forcing doctors and hospitals to perform abortions or other procedures that violate their religious beliefs.

PAGE 8—Section 107(a) makes private health insurance "unlawful," taking away the existing health coverage of approximately 300 million Americans.

PAGE 14—Section 202(a) prohibits cost-sharing, except for a maximum of $200 per year in pharmaceutical co-pays, encouraging over-consumption of "free" care.

PAGE 31—Section 303(c)(2)(B) prohibits any provider who opts out of the single-payer program to care for a single patient from billing that program for *any* service provided to *any* patient for at least one year, a coercive restriction designed to force doctors and hospitals to remain in the government program.

PAGE 47—Section 601(a)(3) contains a mere 58 words directing the secretary of Health and Human Services to determine a "fair allocation" for the national health budget, giving unelected bureaucrats virtually unlimited power over trillions in spending.

PAGE 59—Section 701(b)(3) states that existing restrictions on "any reproductive health service" shall not apply to the new program, overturning more than four decades of bipartisan legislative precedent and allowing for taxpayer-funded abortion-on-demand.

PAGE 63—Section 901(a)(1)(A) states that "no benefits shall be available under Title XVIII of the Social Security Act" once the new single-payer program takes effect, ending the current Medicare program and making the legislation "Medicare for None."

NOWHERE—The legislation contains none of the tax increases necessary to fund its proposed new spending, estimated to cost at least $32 trillion over ten years.

In addition to the provisions included in the reading guide to the House bill, that legislation (H.R. 1384) also includes the provisions described above. However, the House bill may contain slightly different legislative language, and different page numbers.

A READING GUIDE TO H.R. 1384, THE MEDICARE FOR ALL ACT

PAGE 44—Section 401(b)(1)(B)(ii) requires doctors and hospitals to report, as part of an "adequate national database," specific information about health-care employees' hours worked, wage information, and job titles by department—with no protections whatever for employee privacy.

PAGE 63—Section 611 creates a system of global budgets to fund hospitals' quarterly operating expenses, which could cause them to curtail patient care if those lump-sum payments prove insufficient.

PAGE 78—Section 614(b)(2) prohibits federal dollars from subsidizing any profit by medical providers, forcibly destroying tens of billions of dollars of value held by shareholders in these companies, including in Americans' mutual funds and 401(k)s.

PAGE 78—Section 614(b)(4) prohibits federal dollars from subsidizing consultants who educate workers about collective bargaining, stifling providers' First Amendment rights to communicate with their employees.

PAGE 80—Section 614(c)(4) prohibits hospitals from using federal dollars to operate new facilities built with hospitals' own money, confirming that the single-payer system will constrain costs by limiting the available supply of care.

PAGE 81—Section 614(f) prohibits the use of "quality metrics or standards" when reimbursing providers, meaning the government will pay bad doctors and hospitals exactly the same as good ones.

PAGE 84—Section 616(3) requires the secretary of Health and Human Services (HHS) to seize a drug maker's patents if the manufacturer will not agree to an "appropriate price" for the drug, discouraging investors from funding new therapies because their intellectual property could get seized on a bureaucrat's whim.

PAGE 91—Section 701(b)(2)(B) allows the HHS secretary to alter appropriations to the single-payer program in future years, taking the constitutional "power of the purse" away from Congress and putting it in the hands of unelected bureaucrats.

In addition to all the provisions outlined above, the House bill also includes provisions summarized in the reading guide to the Senate bill (S. 1129), albeit in slightly different form and with different page numbers.

introduction

If ever a single day and single event represented the rapid leftward lurch of the Democratic Party, September 13, 2017, would certainly qualify. On that day, in a crowded hearing room in the Hart Senate Office Building, Bernie Sanders, Vermont's socialist senator, reintroduced his single-payer health care legislation.

When he had introduced his single-payer bill at the start of previous Congresses, the launches scarcely attracted notice. No other senator co-sponsored his bill in 2013; in the Congress that ran from 2015 through 2016, Sanders did not even bother to reintroduce single-payer legislation.[1] But after Sanders's upstart presidential campaign took on the Democratic establishment—and elevated the issue of single payer for the far left—his colleagues suddenly showed far more interest.

As *Time* magazine noted on that September day, "a lot more Democrats now back[ed]" the Sanders plan.[2] Including Sanders, a total of 16 Democrats—one-third of the Democrats then serving in the Senate—co-sponsored his bill in the 115th Congress.[3] That list included five Democratic senators who later declared themselves candidates for president in 2020: New Jersey's Cory Booker; New York's Kirsten Gillibrand; California's Kamala Harris; Massachusetts' Elizabeth Warren; and Sanders.[4]

The election of a Democratic majority in the House of Representatives in November 2018 only increased the focus on single payer. A majority of Democrats in that chamber had already endorsed single payer as of 2017.[5] But gaining the House majority led leftist Democrats, including Rep. Pramila Jayapal (D-CA), to go further, asking for, and receiving, a

---

1   S. 1782 (113th Congress), the American Health Security Act of 2013.

2   Nash Jenkins, "A Lot More Democrats Now Back Bernie Sanders's 'Medicare for All' Plan," *Time,* September 13, 2017, http://time.com/4937840/bernie-sanders-health-care-single-payer-medicare-all/.

3   Among the 2017 co-sponsors, Sen. Jeanne Shaheen (D-NH) decided not to co-sponsor Sanders's new bill (S. 1129) in 2019, and Al Franken (D-MN) had resigned from the Senate; all other co-sponsors remained on the legislation.

4   All five again co-sponsored Sanders's bill in 2019.

5   Daniel Marans, "House Democrats See 'Medicare for All' as the Answer to Trumpcare," *Huffington Post* May 24, 2017, https://www.huffpost.com/entry/john-conyers-single-payer-health-care-political-winner_n_5925a104e4b00c8df2a0da51.

commitment from incoming Speaker Nancy Pelosi (D-CA) to hold the first-ever legislative hearings on single payer.[6]

Jayapal reintroduced a single-payer bill in the House in February 2019. The bill followed Sanders's 2017 blueprint, but exceeded it in several respects.[7] The House followed up the bill's introduction with the first-ever hearing on single payer, in the House Rules Committee.[8] The very next day, the Congressional Budget Office released an analysis of the policy choices necessary to create a single-payer system.[9]

But amid all the enthusiasm on the left for single payer, few have bothered to consider the implications of enacting such a major piece of legislation. It would massively disrupt the American health-care system, to say nothing of the United States as a whole.

Consider but a few of the ramifications: Tens of trillions of dollars in new spending—and commensurate tax increases to pay for that spending. The abolition of all private health insurance. Ironically enough for a self-described "Medicare for All" bill, the abolition of the current Medicare program.

---

6   Peter Sullivan, "Pelosi Supports Holding Hearings on 'Medicare for All," *The Hill*, January 3, 2019, https://thehill.com/policy/healthcare/423690-pelosi-supports-holding-congressional-hearings-on-medicare-for-all.

7   Chris Jacobs, "Democrats' New Single Payer Bill Will Destroy Everything Good about Your Health Care," *Federalist*, March 1, 2019, https://thefederalist.com/2019/03/01/democrats-new-single-payer-bill-destroy-everything-good-health-care/.

8   House Rules Committee, Hearing on H.R. 1384, the Medicare for All Act of 2019, April 30, 2019, https://rules.house.gov/hearing/hr-1384-medicare-all-act-2019.

9   Congressional Budget Office, "Key Design Components and Considerations for Establishing a Single Payer Health Care System," May 1, 2019, https://www.cbo.gov/system/files/2019-05/55150-singlepayer.pdf.

Taxpayer-funded abortions, and requirements for doctors and hospitals to perform abortions. Massive increases in government control of our health-care markets. Likely rationing of care as the only means to control skyrocketing costs.

Surveys suggest that support for single payer drops precipitously once individuals understand its downsides.[10] Yet few if any books have taken on single-payer health care to demonstrate its obvious shortcomings. Perhaps conservatives have thought the idea too preposterous or outrageous to believe that the Left would seriously attempt to enact such a wide-ranging, and radical, measure. But as the far-left enthusiasm of the last two years has demonstrated, those days of complacency have long since passed.

This work attempts to make a comprehensive case against single payer. It focuses primarily on two bills: Sanders's legislation in the Senate (S. 1129 of the 116th Congress), and the Jayapal bill (H.R. 1394 of the 116th Congress) in the House. While those bills closely resemble one another, they do contain differences, and the book delineates those where applicable.

It also discusses the various "incremental" bills, some called "Medicare for More," because while they sound more innocuous in nature, they will eventually lead to single payer—not least because their sponsors proclaim that as their goal. Finally, it outlines effective solutions to the problems ailing our current health markets, recognizing that only better alternatives can stave off total government control of health care.

---

10 Ashley Kirzinger, Cailey Munana, and Mollyanne Brodie, "KFF Health Tracking Poll—January 2019: The Public on Next Steps for the ACA and Proposals to Expand Coverage," Kaiser Family Foundation, January 23, 2019, https://www.kff.org/health-reform/poll-finding/kff-health-tracking-poll-january-2019/.

Lest anyone think that references to Sanders in the pages following mean that the Left's movement for single payer will end if and when his 2020 presidential campaign does, think again. In many respects, single payer now represents the mainstream position of the Democratic Party. This work represents one attempt to outline the sizable flaws with that approach, and point a way toward better solutions.

1

IF YOU LIKE YOUR PLAN, YOU CAN'T KEEP IT

KEY POINTS

- Unlike the way President Obama tried to sell Obamacare, liberals have made no attempt to hide the fact that a single-payer system will force people to give up the health coverage they have and like now.

- Whereas a few million people lost their coverage during Obamacare's implementation, a few *hundred million* people would lose their coverage once a single-payer system takes effect.

- Only the 2.3 million Indian Health Service beneficiaries, and 9.3 million enrolled veterans receiving VA benefits, would keep their current health arrangements.

- Even single-payer systems in Canada and Great Britain permit private health insurance offerings, but the House and Senate single-payer bills would make such coverage "unlawful."

- By making it very difficult for individuals to opt out of the government-run system, single payer would force the federal government to fund medical services for everyone, even millionaires, placing enormous pressure on taxpayers, doctors, and the economy.

In an instant viral moment, the American public finally began to sense the audacity, and scope, of liberals' ambitions for our health care. In a town hall broadcast on CNN, presidential candidate Sen. Kamala Harris (D-CA) discussed her co-sponsorship of legislation introduced by Sen. Bernie Sanders to create a single-payer health system. Moderator Jake Tapper asked about provisions in Sanders's bill that would prohibit people from keeping their private insurance coverage. She responded:

> Well listen, the idea is that everyone gets access to medical care. And you don't have to go through the process of going through an insurance company, having them give you approval, going through the paperwork—all of the delay that may require. Who of us has not had that situation, where you've got to wait for approval, and the doctor says, "Well,

I don't know if your insurance company is going to cover this." Let's eliminate all of that. Let's move on.[1]

In other words, if you like your plan, go jump in a lake.[2]

Harris's comments did not surprise analysts who closely follow single-payer legislation. But it shocked plenty of Americans, who may wrongly believe they could keep their coverage under such a system. A January 2019 survey found that 55% of Americans considered participation in such a system "optional."[3] Those numbers echoed an earlier study, conducted in October 2017, which found 47% of Americans—and a majority (52%) of Democrats—believed they could "keep their current health insurance" as part of a "national health plan."[4]

Other polling indicates that support for a single-payer system drops substantially when individuals realize the dramatic implications. A Kaiser Family Foundation poll from January 2019 found that support for single payer fell by 21 percentage points when Americans realized it would "eliminate private health insurance companies." Approval numbers fell even more

---

1   CNN Town Hall with Sen. Kamala Harris, January 28, 2019, http://www.cnn.com/
     TRANSCRIPTS/1901/28/se.01.html.

2   Chris Jacobs, "Kamala Harris Reveals That Medicare for All Involves Ending
     All Private Insurance," *The Federalist*, January 31, 2019, http://thefederalist.
     com/2019/01/31/kamala-harris-reveals-medicare-means-ending-private-insurance/.

3   NORC, "NORC AmeriSpeak Omnibus Survey: Knowledge about Medicare for All
     Remains Low and People's Views Differ on What the Policy Would Do," January 24,
     2019, http://www.norc.org/PDFs/ASonHealth/20190123_MedicareforAll_Topline.
     pdf, p. 5.

4   Ashley Kirzinger, *et al.*, "Data Note: Public's Views of a National Health Plan,"
     Kaiser Family Foundation, October 25, 2017, https://www.kff.org/health-reform/
     poll-finding/data-note-publics-views-of-a-national-health-plan/.

when interviewers suggested that the plan would require sizable tax increases (23%), jeopardize the current Medicare program (28%), or lead to delays in accessing treatment (44%).[5]

The organization that conducted the survey, the Kaiser Family Foundation, has a decidedly liberal bent. For instance, Kaiser surveys have touted Obamacare's benefits while minimizing the law's costs and drawbacks.[6] That even a liberal organization found such a dramatic change in public opinion on single payer speaks to the disquiet among Americans when they discover the true implications of such a scheme.

BARACK OBAMA'S "LIE OF THE YEAR"

Not so long ago, Democrats felt the need to reassure Americans that they would *not* lose their current coverage. When selling his health plan on the presidential campaign trail in 2008, and while trying to convince Congress to pass Obamacare in 2009 and 2010, Barack Obama repeatedly promised Americans that "If you like your plan, you can keep it." One video shows Obama making that pledge on 36 separate occasions.[7]

---

5   Ashley Kirzinger, Cailey Munana, and Mollyanne Brodie, "KFF Health Tracking Poll—January 2019: The Public on Next Steps for the ACA and Proposals to Expand Coverage," Kaiser Family Foundation, January 23, 2019, https://www.kff.org/health-reform/poll-finding/kff-health-tracking-poll-january-2019/.

6   Chris Jacobs, "*Politico* Reporter's 'Fact Check' on President Trump on Health Care Is Riddled with Omissions," *The Federalist,* September 24, 2018, http://thefederalist.com/2018/09/24/politico-reporters-fact-check-president-trump-health-care-riddled-errors/; Chris Jacobs, "What Liberals Won't Tell You about Pre-Existing Conditions," *The Federalist,* June 28, 2018, http://thefederalist.com/2018/06/28/liberals-wont-tell-pre-existing-conditions/.

7   "36 Times Obama Said You Could Keep Your Health Care Plan," *Washington Free Beacon,* November 5, 2013, https://www.youtube.com/watch?v=qpa-5JdCnmo.

Obama made his "like your plan" promise in large part because similar concerns had helped sink "Hillarycare"—the health-care proposal put forward by Bill and Hillary Clinton in 1993-94. The famous "Harry and Louise" ad campaign at the time warned that "the government may force us to pick from a few health care plans designed by government bureaucrats"; one ad ended with the refrain, "They choose—we lose."[8] Mindful of the implosion of the Clinton plan under a Democratic Congress, Obama felt the need to provide constant reassurance that his legislation would not upset Americans' current arrangements.

Of course, Obama's promise ended up proving untrue, as few Americans can forget. At least 4.7 million Americans received cancellation notices in 2013, when insurers started ripping up old policies before Obamacare's major provisions took effect in January 2014.[9] But with healthcare.gov in an online meltdown—Kathleen Sebelius, Obama's own secretary of Health and Human Services, called the website a "debacle"—these individuals lost their existing plans with no ability to buy a replacement.[10]

Eventually, Obama offered an apology for the "like your plan" fiasco. In a November 2013 interview, he said, "I am sorry that [people] are finding themselves in this situation based on

---

8   "Harry and Louise on Clinton's Health Plan," https://www.youtube.com/watch?v=Dt31nhleeCg.

9   Associated Press, "Policy Notifications and Current Status, by State," December 26, 2013, https://finance.yahoo.com/news/policy-notifications-current-status-state-204701399.html.

10   David Nather, "Sebelius Struggles to Clean Up," *Politico*, October 30, 2013, https://www.politico.com/story/2013/10/kathleen-sebelius-obamacare-099115.

assurances they got from me."[11] He issued his apology in the face of unstinting criticism. PolitiFact called the "If you like your plan" pledge its "Lie of the Year" for 2013.[12] The administration attempted to save face, and help Americans struggling to find replacement coverage, by allowing states to keep certain plans intact, even though some legal experts believe Obama (and President Trump after him) violated their constitutional duties to uphold the law by keeping these plans in place.[13]

But as the saying goes, that was then, and this is now. While just a few years ago, President Obama went to great—what some have called unconstitutional—lengths to avoid cancelling the insurance policies of a few million individuals as Obamacare went into effect, the single-payer legislation that many Democratic presidential candidates now support would cancel the insurance coverage of a few *hundred million* Americans.

11   Chuck Todd, "Exclusive: Obama Personally Apologizes for Americans Losing Health Coverage," NBC News, November 7, 2013, https://www.nbcnews.com/news/us-news/exclusive-obama-personally-apologizes-americans-losing-health-coverage-flna8C11555216.

12   Angie Drobnic Holan, "Lie of the Year: 'If You Like Your Health Care Plan, You Can Keep It,'" *PolitiFact,* December 12, 2013, https://www.politifact.com/truth-o-meter/article/2013/dec/12/lie-year-if-you-like-your-health-care-plan-keep-it/.

13   Centers for Medicare and Medicaid Services, Letter to State Insurance Commissioners regarding transitional plan arrangements, November 14, 2013, https://www.cms.gov/CCIIO/Resources/Letters/Downloads/commissioner-letter-11-14-2013.PDF; Nicholas Bagley, "Legal Limits and the Implementation of the Affordable Care Act," *University of Pennsylvania Law Review,* December 1, 2016, https://papers.ssrn.com/sol3/papers.cfm?abstract_id=2721391, pp. 1722-23.

WHO WOULD LOSE THEIR PLANS—AND WHY

Section 107 of the House and Senate bills makes clear that under a single-payer system, the government health plan will serve as the only option for Americans' health coverage:

> (a) IN GENERAL.—Beginning on the effective date described in section 106(a), it shall be unlawful for—
>
> (1) a private health insurer to sell health insurance coverage that duplicates the benefits provided under this Act; or
>
> (2) an employer to provide benefits for an employee, former employee, or the dependents of an employee or former employee that duplicate the benefits provided under this Act.[14]

The legislation prescribes a health coverage "Big Bang"— an effective date, two years after enactment in the House bill, and four years after enactment in the Senate bill, after which all existing health coverage "shall be unlawful." Yet, ironically enough, Sanders claims that his bill offers "freedom of choice."[15] If making coverage "unlawful" constitutes "freedom of choice," just imagine what coercion might look like.

When calculating who would lose their current coverage under single payer, it makes more sense to delineate the few people allowed to keep their existing arrangements. Section 901(d) provides that nothing in the House and Senate bills "shall affect the eligibility of veterans for the medical benefits and services" provided by the Department of Veterans Affairs,

---

14   Section 107(a) of H.R. 1384 and S. 1129, the Medicare for All Act of 2019.

15   Holly Otterbein, "Sanders Takes on Fox—And Emerges Triumphant," *Politico,* April 15, 2019, https://www.politico.com/story/2019/04/15/bernie-sanders-millionaire-no-apology-1277009.

"or of Indians for the medical benefits and services provided by or through the Indian Health Service."[16] According to the most recent data, approximately 9.3 million enrolled veterans receive care through the VA, and 2.3 million Native Americans receive coverage through the Indian Health Service.[17] *Only* these individuals could keep their existing health coverage under current single-payer proposals.

As to who would lose their health coverage, those totals include the following:

1. Americans with employer coverage: 181 million[18]

2. Individuals with Obamacare coverage, whether purchased on or off of the law's insurance exchanges: 14.4 million[19]

---

16   Section 901(d) of H.R. 1384 and S. 1129.

17   Department of Veterans Affairs, "Fiscal Year 2020 Budget in Brief," March 2019, https://www.va.gov/budget/docs/summary/fy2020VAbudgetInBrief.pdf; Indian Health Service, "IHS Profile," Departmental fact sheet, July 2018, https://www.ihs.gov/newsroom/factsheets/ihsprofile/.

18   Edward Berchick, Emily Hood, and Jessica Barnett, "Health Insurance Coverage in the United States: 2017," Census Bureau Report P60-264, September 2018, https://www.census.gov/content/dam/Census/library/publications/2018/demo/p60-264.pdf, Table 1, Coverage Numbers and Rates by Type of Health Insurance: 2013, 2016, and 2017, p. 4.

19   Ashley Semanskee, Larry Levitt, and Cynthia Cox, "Data Note: Changes in Enrollment in the Individual Health Insurance Market," Kaiser Family Foundation, July 31, 2018, https://www.kff.org/health-reform/issue-brief/data-note-changes-in-enrollment-in-the-individual-health-insurance-market/.

3. Those enrolled in Medicaid and the State Children's Health Insurance Program: 72.5 million[20]

4. Tricare enrollees: 9.4 million active and retired military service members and their families[21]

5. Participants in the Federal Employee Health Benefits Program: 8.2 million workers and retirees[22]

6. Medicare beneficiaries: 60.4 million[23]

Some of the above numbers overlap—because Tricare and the Federal Employee Health Benefits Program also qualify as employer coverage, and because individuals may hold multiple forms of coverage (e.g., Medicare and Medicaid, or Medicare and coverage from a former employer). But of 323 million Americans, only about 11 million in the VA or Indian Health Service systems would retain their current health arrangements.[24]

---

20 Centers for Medicare and Medicaid Services, "December 2018 Medicaid and CHIP Enrollment Data Highlights," https://www.medicaid.gov/medicaid/program-information/medicaid-and-chip-enrollment-data/report-highlights/index.html. Unlike the House bill, Section 204 of S. 1129 would keep a limited role for state Medicaid programs in providing institutional long-term care (i.e., nursing home) services. However, in both the House and Senate bills, the federal single-payer program would assume delivery of all *health care* services for Medicaid beneficiaries.

21 Defense Health Agency, "Tricare: Number of Beneficiaries," January 4, 2019, https://www.tricare.mil/About/Facts/BeneNumbers.aspx.

22 Alan Spielman, "Federal Benefits Open Season Begins," Office of Personnel Management Director's blog, November 16, 2017, https://www.opm.gov/blogs/Director/2017/11/16/Federal-Benefits-Open-Season-Begins/.

23 Centers for Medicare and Medicaid Services, "Medicare Enrollment Dashboard," December 2018, https://www.cms.gov/Research-Statistics-Data-and-Systems/Statistics-Trends-and-Reports/Dashboard/Medicare-Enrollment/Enrollment%20Dashboard.html.

24 Berchick, "Health Insurance Coverage," Table 1, p. 4.

In addition, because the newest version of the House legislation also includes benefits for long-term care, the 7.2 million individuals who purchased long-term care insurance will also see their coverage cancelled.[25] For instance, my mother purchased a long-term care insurance policy some years ago, to provide both me and her financial protection should she ever need nursing home care. Although she has paid tens of thousands of dollars in premiums on the policy over several decades, passage of the House single-payer bill would render her policy worthless and "unlawful."

While Americans have concerns about U.S. health care markets, most like their existing insurance plans and have for quite some time. In November 2018, a Gallup poll found that nearly seven in ten Americans considered their health coverage either excellent (27%) or good (42%).[26] Over the 18 years Gallup has conducted the survey, the number of Americans considering their health coverage either good or excellent has never slipped below 63%.[27]

---

25   Section 204 of H.R. 1384; Marc Cohen, "The State of the Long-Term Care Insurance Market," in National Association of Insurance Commissioners, *The State of Long-Term Care Insurance: The Market, Challenges, and Future Innovations*, May 2016, https://naic.org/documents/cipr_current_study_160519_ltc_insurance.pdf, Table 1, Key Industry Parameters, p. 8. The Senate bill would subsume home and community-based services—but NOT institutional long-term care services—into the single-payer program, making the status of privately purchased long-term care policies under that regime unclear.

26   Gallup, "Health Care System," https://news.gallup.com/poll/4708/healthcare-system.aspx.

27   Ibid.

OPTING OUT NOT REALLY AN OPTION

Would patients still have an opportunity to opt out of the single-payer system, notwithstanding the prohibition on private insurance coverage for any benefit provided by the government system? With single payer, the exception may prove the power of the rule.

The single-payer bills do allow providers to opt out of the government system, but at a very high cost. While the specifics vary in the House and Senate bills, both pieces of legislation would prohibit providers who participate in the government system from entering into *any* private contract with *any* eligible individual for *any* covered item or service.[28] Providers wishing to contract privately must obtain written consent in which patients must agree to accept full financial responsibility for those services—and providers must agree not to participate in the government system *at all.*[29]

To put it another way, patients who want private care must find a doctor who treats private patients *only,* because physicians who operate in the government system cannot treat patients privately, period, except for non-covered services like cosmetic surgery. This restriction far exceeds those in place in Britain's single-payer health system, where doctors who work for the National Health Service (NHS) during the day can and

---

28 Section 303 of H.R. 1384 and S. 1129.

29 Ibid. Section 303(b) of the House bill contains provisions allowing participating providers to provide non-covered services to patients via private contracts, provided appropriate disclosure occurs. However, because the government system prescribes a very generous benefit package, it appears that providers would have few opportunities to provide non-covered services, cosmetic surgery being the sole likely scenario.

do moonlight as private practitioners, without giving up their right to participate in the government system.[30]

Given the onerous restrictions on private contracting included in the House and Senate single-payer legislation, several likely scenarios follow should either bill get enacted into law:

1. *Some individuals would likely decide to opt out of the government system for physician care.* Some doctors do not accept Medicare, or indeed any form of health insurance. Whether called "concierge" medicine or direct primary care, these types of practices have grown since Obamacare's enactment.[31] Many charge their patients a set fee (for instance, $50-100 per month) for an unlimited number of visits, whether in-person or virtual. The growing market for this type of care, notwithstanding the fact that many providers do not accept insurance, suggests that at least some of these practices could survive the transition to a single-payer system.

2. *However, few if any individuals could afford to opt out of the government system completely.* While many families could pay for their physician care—which generally costs no more than a few thousand dollars per year—out-of-pocket, few could fund more intense conditions themselves. Expensive drugs and long hospital stays can easily cost into the millions, such that most people would find

---

30 David Oliver, "Private Practice by NHS Doctors—Still Controversial?" *BMJ,* August 14, 2018, https://www.bmj.com/content/362/bmj.k3480.

31 Shefali Luthra, "Fueled by Health Law, 'Concierge Medicine' Reaches New Markets," *Kaiser Health News,* January 14, 2016, https://khn.org/news/fueled-by-health-law-concierge-medicine-reaches-new-markets/.

it difficult to fund all their health expenses—because by law, insurance could not absorb the burden of these costly episodes. The high wall between the government system and private practice would also discourage people from opting out: Anyone who contracts with a private doctor for direct primary care could not have that doctor care for him if he ended up in a government-funded hospital.

3. *Few if any hospitals could afford to opt out of the government system.* Because few individuals can afford to fund hospital care out-of-pocket, hospitals wishing to remain outside the government system would have few available customers to fund their operations. A few clinics might remain, for elective cosmetic surgery or to fund care for ultra-wealthy individuals, but the vast majority of hospitals would likely have no choice but to participate in the government system.

These restrictions, and the implications of them, raise obvious questions. If single payer will produce the socialist paradise Sanders and his supporters claim, why do they impose so many restrictions on people who wish to opt out of the system? Does Sanders want to compel millionaires to use the government-run health program as a form of punishment?

An obscure tidbit of history provides a useful analogy to the restrictions on private contracting in the single-payer bills. The barrier around the German capital that Western democracies called the Berlin Wall had a far different name in Communist-run East Germany: The Anti-Fascist Protection Rampart. Despite all the obvious evidence to the contrary, the East German government claimed that the wall they built functioned not to imprison their citizens, but to keep others from entering the country to enjoy the Communist "paradise." Perhaps Sanders, who has a rhapsodic history with the Communist Eastern Bloc, borrowed this idea from the East Germans—to prevent few Americans from missing the "joy" of his socialist "paradise."[32]

Regardless of the motivation behind these restrictions on private contracting, it seems clear that even millionaires, and some multi-millionaires, will likely have to use the single-payer system for at least some of their health needs. Billionaires such as Mark Zuckerberg can afford to pay out-of-pocket for all their health care, no matter its cost. (Zuckerberg could build a hospital just to treat himself, if he wished.) But individuals with a net worth of $1 million, or even $5 million or $10 million, could not afford to fund all their care themselves if they got leukemia or their family was involved in a horrible car crash.

Liberals see this characteristic of single payer as a feature: All, or nearly all, individuals would receive the same care, under the same system. But common sense would view this movement for universality as a bug. After all, creating a single-payer system would require more than doubling current federal income tax rates.[33] Why should individuals of modest means, who almost certainly will have to pay some of the costs associated with this massive new government scheme, face higher taxes so the federal

32   Michael Kranish, "Inside Bernie Sanders' 1988 10-day 'Honeymoon' in the Soviet Union," *Washington Post*, May 3, 2019, https://www.washingtonpost.com/politics/inside-bernie-sanderss-1988-10-day-honeymoon-in-the-soviet-union/2019/05/02/db543e18-6a9c-11e9-a66d-a82d3f3d96d5_story.html?utm_term=.220bf92174da.

33   Charles Blahous, "The Costs of a National Single Payer Health Care System," Mercatus Center, July 30, 2018, https://www.mercatus.org/system/files/blahous-costs-medicare-mercatus-working-paper-v1_1.pdf.

government can fund the health care of millionaires and other people in the "one percent"?

THE BILL'S RADICAL NATURE

In banning private insurance outright, Democrats' single-payer bill would far exceed practices in other countries, even countries with single-payer systems. Great Britain, for instance, permits private health insurance, which has fairly widespread take-up. As of 2015, just more than 10% of the population held private health insurance, 3.94 million policies in all.[34] Some employers provide private insurance as a benefit to their workers, while other individuals purchase coverage themselves.[35] Either way, private insurance provides supplemental benefits, whether paying for drugs that the NHS will not cover, or funding care—such as specialist consultations or non-emergency surgery—subject to long waits within the government-run system.[36]

Likewise, Canada's single-payer system, also called Medicare, relies heavily on private health insurance. All told, about 25 million Canadians, or roughly two-thirds of Canada's population,

34 Quoted in Ruth Thorlby and Sandeepa Arora, "The English Health Care System," in Elias Mossialos, *et al.*, eds., *International Profiles of Health Care Systems*, Commonwealth Fund, May 2017, https://www.commonwealthfund.org/sites/default/files/documents/___media_files_publications_fund_report_2017_may_mossialos_intl_profiles_v5.pdf, p. 49.

35 Robert Wachter, "The Awkward World of Private Insurance in the U.K.," *The Health Care Blog*, January 16, 2012, https://thehealthcareblog.com/blog/2012/01/16/the-awkward-world-of-private-insurance-in-the-uk/.

36 King's Fund, "The UK Private Health Care Market: Appendix to the Commission on the Future of Health and Social Care in England," 2014, https://www.kingsfund.org.uk/sites/default/files/media/commission-appendix-uk-private-health-market.pdf.

hold some form of private health coverage.[37] Because Canada's federal government does not require provincial health systems to cover outpatient prescription drugs, most individuals obtain some form of health insurance to fund these and other supplemental benefits.[38]

Unlike the health plans funded by the Canadian and British governments, the single-payer system proposed by Sanders and Rep. Pramila Jayapal presumes to provide every possible service to every American, and at no out-of-pocket cost to them, giving the sponsors their justification to ban private health insurance. But over and above the philosophical issues associated with banning private health insurance—Why shouldn't individuals be able to buy supplemental or private coverage if they want it?—comes an important logistical question: Can a government-run system cope on its own?

The examples of countries like Canada and Britain suggest that a system that banned private health insurance entirely would face two complementary problems. Would the government system have the money, and the capacity, to fund all medical procedures for all individuals? One American health care expert wrote that he didn't understand the need for private insurance in Britain, until an NHS manager explained that private care provides a pressure-relief valve for the government-run system:

---

37 Canadian Life and Health Insurance Association, "Canadian Life and Health Insurance Facts: 2018 Edition," https://www.clhia.ca/web/clhia_lp4w_lnd_webstation.nsf/resources/Factbook_2/$file/2018+FB+EN.pdf, p. 14.

38 Sara Allin and David Rudoler, "The Canadian Health Care System," in Mossialos, *et al.*, *International Profiles*, pp. 21-22.

IF YOU LIKE YOUR PLAN, YOU CAN'T KEEP IT

All the people using the private system have already paid their taxes, so they are siphoning volume out of the NHS that the system otherwise would have to manage....*The NHS would come to a grinding halt if private practice went away.*[39] [Emphasis added.]

By banning private insurance outright, the single-payer bills would not just infringe on American citizens' freedom to buy the health coverage they desire. That prohibition would also place tremendous financial and capacity pressures on the government-run system, which it likely could not handle.

MORE GOVERNMENT IS NOT THE ANSWER

In 2000, the late-night show *Saturday Night Live* broadcast a famous sketch, entitled "More Cowbell," in which a record producer played by Christopher Walken asks the band Blue Oyster Cult to "crank up" the cowbell sound in the recording studio. Walken's character says: "I got a fever—and the only prescription is more cowbell."[40]

That "more cowbell" attitude describes liberals' attitude about government size to a T. To them, liberals' belief in "progress" means an ever-expanding role for government. As Ronald Reagan famously quipped about the Left's view of the economy: "If it moves, tax it. If it keeps moving, regulate it. And if it stops moving, subsidize it."

Having passed Obamacare with 60 votes in the Senate, Democrats could have put *whatever* they wanted into the legislation to control health-care costs. Yet premiums continue to rise

---

39   Wachter, "The Awkward World."

40   Video available at https://www.youtube.com/watch?v=cVsQLlk-T0s.

inexorably higher: More than 2.5 million individuals dropped Obamacare plans in one year alone, most because they could not afford their premiums.[41]

In view of this clear failure, what do Obamacare supporters propose? More spending on subsidies and more regulation of insurers and prices, or proposals for an entirely government-run system. Government caused the problem, so obviously more government will lead to a solution!

Therein lies the left's siren call: *Just give us more power, and we'll solve all your problems for you.* Yet somehow, the power the Left receives always proves insufficient to accomplish its stated goals.[42]

The single-payer plan amounts to liberals' most audacious power grab yet: taking away the health coverage of nearly 300 million Americans. One-fifth of them—the seniors and individuals with disabilities covered by the current Medicare program—may especially find "Medicare for All" much less alluring than its proponents want them to believe.

---

41 Semanskee, Levitt, and Cox, "Changes in Enrollment."

42 Chris Jacobs, "Obama-Supporting Think Tank Admits Obamacare Has Failed, Recommends Doubling Down," *The Federalist,* July 20, 2018, http://thefederalist.com/2018/07/20/obama-supporting-think-tank-admits-obamacare-failed-recommends-doubling/.

2

"MEDICARE FOR NONE" WILL HARM SENIORS

KEY POINTS

- Despite claims it would provide "Medicare for All," single-payer legislation would abolish the current Medicare program and liquidate the Medicare trust funds, making the program "Medicare for None."

- In closing the existing Medicare program and creating a new one that also uses the Medicare name, single-payer supporters claim seniors would be better off. In reality, however, the transition would seriously harm seniors.

- Nearly 23 million Medicare beneficiaries would lose access to the Medicare Advantage plans they have, and like. These plans often provide more benefits and better care to seniors than traditional Medicare, but because the single-payer bills make private health insurance "unlawful," these plans would be abolished.

- In addition, the single-payer bills take dollars from the Medicare program—already running sizable financial shortfalls—and transfer them into a single-payer program with an even less secure funding base.

- As with Obamacare, the Left considers Medicare a piggy bank to raid to pay for expanding health benefits to people other than seniors.

- Because even wealthy individuals will likely be unable to entirely opt out of government-run single payer, the single-payer bills effectively take money from low-income seniors to fund health care for the wealthy.

- If the United States does not set clear priorities for who can claim others' earnings, our country will become unable to care for those who need it most, especially seniors and the most vulnerable.

Sen. Bernie Sanders and supporters of single-payer health care have tried to sell their legislation as creating "Medicare for All." But Section 901(a) of the House and Senate single-payer bills reveals some problems with the accuracy of that assertion:

> (1) IN GENERAL.—Notwithstanding any other provision of law...

(A) no benefits shall be available under title XVIII of the Social Security Act for any item or service furnished beginning on [the effective date of the new program—two years after enactment in the House bill, and four years after enactment in the Senate bill].[1]

Title XVIII of the Social Security Act refers to Medicare, created as part of the Social Security Act Amendments of 1965, meaning this section of the legislation ends Americans' entitlement to the current Medicare program.[2] Section 701 of the House and Senate bills liquidates the dollars currently in the Medicare trust funds:

(d) TRANSFER OF FUNDS.—Any amounts remaining in the Federal Hospital Insurance Trust Fund…or the Federal Supplementary Medical Insurance Trust…after the payment of claims for items and services furnished under title XVIII of such Act have been completed, shall be transferred into the Universal Medicare Trust Fund under this section.[3]

These financial maneuverings reveal that the authors of single payer haven't proposed expanding the current Medicare program to all Americans so much as abolishing it and instituting a new program. In short, instead of proposing "Medicare for All," Sanders has proposed "Medicare for None."[4]

---

1 Section 901(a)(1) of H.R. 1384 and S. 1129, the Medicare for All Act of 2019.

2 P.L. 89-97, as subsequently amended.

3 Section 701(d) of H.R. 1384 and S. 1129.

4 Chris Jacobs, "Sanders Proposes Medicare for None," *The Wall Street Journal* January 18, 2018, https://www.wsj.com/articles/sanders-proposes-medicare-for-none-1516233970.

Single-payer supporters might call this criticism little more than a silly argument over semantics. Sure, the legislation liquidates the current Medicare trust funds, but seniors—along with all Americans—will have access to better benefits than the current Medicare program provides. Who should complain about that?

First off, this kind of sleight-of-hand is inherently dishonest, and disingenuous. If Sanders wants to create a new program, he should say so outright, and call it for what it is. That he will not—just like Barack Obama knew, but would not admit, that some people would not be able to keep their health plans—speaks to the deceptive ways liberal politicians must sell their agenda to voters.[5]

But Sanders's lack of candor about the true effects of his single-payer bill may well stem from *understanding* how its policies would harm current Medicare enrollees. Millions of seniors will lose the private health plans they have now, which provide more coordinated, and arguably better, care than the government-run Medicare plan.

Moreover, shifting dollars from the current Medicare program to fund the new national program undermines a promise made to seniors. Yes, the current Medicare program has funding shortfalls, which Congress should address urgently. But taking current Medicare dollars and diverting them into a larger scheme—the $30 trillion-plus cost of which liberals have little idea how to fund—betrays those trusting their elderly years to this long-running government program.

---

5   Lisa Myers and Hannah Rappleye, "Obama Administration Knew Millions Could Not Keep Their Health Insurance," NBC News, October 29, 2013, https://www. nbcnews.com/news/world/obama-administration-knew-millions-could-not-keep-their-health-insurance-flna8C11485678.

As the last chapter discussed, the House and Senate single-payer bills' prohibition on private health insurance means that wealthy individuals, and even many millionaires, will not be able to opt out of the new government-run system. By liquidating the current Medicare trust funds, the single-payer bills would effectively take dollars from indigent seniors to fund the health care of affluent millionaires.

SENIORS LOSING COVERAGE

A large, and growing, number of seniors receive Medicare benefits not through the government-run Medicare plan, but through Medicare Advantage plans. These privately run insurance plans—whether Health Maintenance Organizations (HMOs), Preferred Provider Organizations (PPOs), or special-needs plans for individuals with chronic conditions—deliver to enrollees the Medicare benefits prescribed by law, and often other benefits. The plans provide coordinated care for beneficiaries, and closely resemble the employer-based HMO and PPO plans that many individuals held prior to retirement.

As of 2019, Medicare Advantage plans enrolled 22.8 million beneficiaries—more than one-third (37.8%) of the 61.3 million beneficiaries enrolled in Medicare.[6] The Medicare actuary projects that over the next decade, Medicare Advantage enrollment will continue to rise—both in absolute terms, and as a percentage of overall Medicare enrollees. By 2028, Medicare Advantage

---

6   Centers for Medicare and Medicaid Services, "2019 Annual Report of the Boards of Trustees of the Federal Hospital Insurance and Federal Supplemental Medical Insurance Trust Funds," April 22, 2019, https://www.cms.gov/Research-Statistics-Data-and-Systems/Statistics-Trends-and-Reports/ReportsTrustFunds/Downloads/TR2019.pdf?mod=article_inline, Table IV.C1, Private Health Plan Enrollment, p. 148.

enrollment will reach an estimated 30.7 million seniors, or 40% of the estimated 76.7 million Medicare beneficiaries.[7]

Ironically, Medicare Advantage enrollment has continued to rise in recent years, even after Obamacare significantly reduced payments to Advantage plans. According to Congressional Budget Office estimates at the time of the law's enactment, Obamacare would reduce Medicare Advantage payments by $205.9 billion from 2010 through 2019.[8] At the time, the Medicare actuary predicted that these payment reductions would cause Advantage enrollment to decline from 11.7 million, and 24.7% of all Medicare enrollees, in 2010 to 8.2 million enrollees, and only 13.2% of the entire Medicare population, in 2019.[9]

Medicare Advantage has gained in popularity, rather than losing enrollees after Obamacare's reductions to the program, in large part because it provides better benefits to seniors.[10] Study after study demonstrates the advantages of the privately run Medicare Advantage:

---

7   Ibid.

8   Congressional Budget Office, Cost Estimate for H.R. 4872 (Final Health Care
     Legislation), March 20, 2010, https://www.cbo.gov/sites/default/files/111th-
     congress-2009-2010/costestimate/amendreconprop.pdf, Table 5, Estimate of
     the Effects of Non-Coverage Health Provisions of the Reconciliation Proposal
     Combined with H.R. 3590 as Passed by the Senate, p. 27 and p. 32.

9   Centers for Medicare and Medicaid Services, "2010 Annual Report of the Boards
     of Trustees of the Federal Hospital Insurance and Federal Supplemental Medical
     Insurance Trust Funds," August 5, 2010, https://www.cms.gov/Research-Statistics-
     Data-and-Systems/Statistics-Trends-and-Reports/ReportsTrustFunds/Downloads/
     TR2010.pdf, Table IV.C1, Private Health Plan Enrollment, p. 198.

10   Much of the research in the following section was originally conducted by
     Christopher Pope in "Enhancing Medicare Advantage," Manhattan Institute,
     February 28, 2019, https://media4.manhattan-institute.org/sites/default/files/
     R-CP-0219.pdf.

- *More Coordinated Care*: After adjusting for demographics and health risk factors, Medicare Advantage enrollees have a lower-than-expected death rate than beneficiaries in traditional Medicare—with the lower mortality rates most pronounced among minorities and those with multiple health conditions.[11] That mortality gap may stem from the fact that Medicare Advantage enrollees at risk for diseases such as breast cancer and diabetes were more likely to receive appropriate tests, and to receive preventive treatments like vaccinations for influenza and pneumonia.[12] Advantage enrollees are also 43% less likely to die in the hospital, making them more likely to die a peaceful death at home—the kind of death most Americans would prefer.[13]

- *Fewer Hospitalizations*: Medicare Advantage enrollees are 7% less likely to have surgery on an inpatient basis, and 26% more likely to have surgery on an outpatient

---

11   Roy A. Beveridge, *et al.*, "Mortality Differences Between Traditional Medicare and Medicare Advantage," *Inquiry,* June 2017, https://journals.sagepub.com/doi/pdf/10.1177/0046958017709103.

12   John Z. Ayanian, "Medicare Beneficiaries More Likely to Receive Appropriate Ambulatory Services in HMOs than in Traditional Medicare," *Health Affairs,* July 2013, https://www.healthaffairs.org/doi/full/10.1377/hlthaff.2012.0773.

13   Elizabeth E. Chen and Edward A. Miller, "A Longitudinal Analysis of Site of Death: The Effects of Continuous Enrollment in Medicare Advantage Versus Conventional Medicare," *Research on Aging,* September 2017, https://journals.sagepub.com/doi/abs/10.1177/0164027516645843?journalCode=roaa; David G. Stevenson, "Service Use at the End of Life in Medicare Advantage versus Traditional Medicare," *Medical Care,* October 2013, https://www.ncbi.nlm.nih.gov/pmc/articles/PMC3804008/.

basis.[14] Medicare Advantage's greater usage of outpatient surgery compared to inpatient procedures not only saves costs; it gets patients home sooner while reducing the risk of adverse events, like a hospital-acquired infection. Advantage patients also have 20-25% fewer inpatient admissions than patients in traditional Medicare, and 25-35% fewer emergency room visits.[15] And patients who leave Advantage to join traditional Medicare had a 60% increase in hospital use, without any improvement in quality or mortality, suggesting that Advantage plans do a better job of coordinating care in ways that prevent unnecessary, or low-value, health spending.[16]

- *Better Benefits*: Because plans must return savings back to beneficiaries in the form of lower costs or enhanced benefits, seniors see the results in their wallets. Nine in ten (90%) Medicare beneficiaries can access a Medicare Advantage prescription drug plan without a monthly premium—and more than half (55%) of Advantage enrollees

---

14   Vilsa Curto *et al.*, "Health Care Spending and Utilization in Public and Private Medicare," National Bureau of Economic Research Working Paper 23090, January 2017, http://www.nber.org/papers/w23090.pdf.

15   Bruce E. Landon, *et al.*, "Analysis of Medicare Advantage HMOs Compared with Traditional Medicare Shows Lower Use of Many Services During 2003–09," *Health Affairs,* December 2012, https://www.healthaffairs.org/doi/full/10.1377/hlthaff.2012.0179.

16   Mark Duggan, Jonathan Gruber, and Boris Vabson, "The Consequences of Health Care Privatization: Evidence from Medicare Advantage Exits," *American Economic Journal,* February 2018, https://dspace.mit.edu/openaccess-disseminate/1721.1/114042.

do so.[17] Advantage enrollees also receive more generous coverage of their prescription drugs than do enrollees in traditional Medicare.[18] And large numbers of Advantage enrollees have signed up for plans that offer supplemental eye exams (77%), fitness benefits (69%), and dental coverage (62%).[19]

- *Greater Efficiency:* Medicare Advantage enrollees have 10-25% lower spending than enrollees in traditional Medicare in the same county, even after controlling for differences in health status.[20]

- *Lower Spending in Traditional Medicare:* A 1% increase in Medicare Advantage plan penetration in a given area leads to an average 1.7% reduction in spending for enrollees in traditional Medicare, as well as fewer and shorter hospital stays for traditional Medicare patients.[21] An increase in Medicare Advantage plan penetration also leads to shorter

---

17 Medicare Payment Advisory Commission, *Report to the Congress: Medicare Payment Policy,* March 15, 2019, http://medpac.gov/docs/default-source/reports/mar19_medpac_entirereport_sec.pdf?sfvrsn=0, Table 13-2, Access to Medicare Advantage Plans Remains High, p. 353.

18 Amanda Starc and Robert J. Town, "Externalities and Benefit Design in Health Insurance," National Bureau of Economic Research Working Paper 21783, April 2018, http://www.nber.org/papers/w21783.pdf.

19 Gretchen Jacobson, Anthony Damico, and Tricia Neuman, "A Dozen Facts about Medicare Advantage," Kaiser Family Foundation data note, November 13, 2018, https://www.kff.org/medicare/issue-brief/a-dozen-facts-about-medicare-advantage/.

20 Curto, *et al.,* "Health Care Spending and Utilization."

21 Yevgeniy Feyman and Austin Frakt, "The Persistence of Medicare Advantage Spillovers in the Post-Affordable Care Act Era," SSRN Working Paper 3072604, November 16, 2017, https://papers.ssrn.com/sol3/papers.cfm?abstract_id=3072604.

hospital stays, and a decrease in overall hospital spending, for non-Medicare patients.[22] Medicare Advantage growth leads doctors and hospitals to improve care coordination, yielding positive benefits for the health of an entire region.

Critics claim that Medicare Advantage plans game the system, either by selecting healthier patients, or via healthier patients who self-select into Medicare Advantage, giving the private program an unfair edge.[23] However, that claim misses an important point: If some individuals do self-select into Medicare Advantage, that selection only occurs because government bureaucrats have (unsurprisingly) made government-run Medicare the default option for seniors. Medicare Advantage plans could provide infinitely better care to seniors at a much lower cost—but do such considerations matter more than the leftist ideology that proclaims, "Government good, private bad?" Of course not.

The liberal criticism speaks to the Left's inherent bias in favor of government-run care, and against private options. First they sabotage private plans, by making it tougher for them to enroll seniors. Then they attack the plans by criticizing the seniors Medicare Advantage insurers do get to enroll. If you think this system seems rigged against private insurance and in

---

22   Katherine Baicker, Michael Chernew, and Jacob Robbins, "The Spillover Effects of Medicare Managed Care: Medicare Advantage and Hospital Utilization," National Bureau of Economic Research Working Paper 19070, May 2013, http://www.nber.org/papers/w19070.pdf.

23   Gretchen Jacobson, Tricia Neuman, and Anthony Damico, "Do People Who Sign Up for Medicare Advantage Plans Have Lower Medicare Spending?" Kaiser Family Foundation issue brief, May 7, 2019, https://www.kff.org/medicare/issue-brief/do-people-who-sign-up-for-medicare-advantage-plans-have-lower-medicare-spending/.

favor of government-run Medicare, you'd be correct.

Liberal attacks notwithstanding, most evidence strongly suggests that Medicare Advantage's coordinated care provides better benefits at a lower cost. Most seniors see many physicians, but Medicare Advantage plans do a better job of coordinating care—making sure the primary care physician speaks to, and works closely with, specialists like the cardiologist treating a patient's heart failure, or the orthopedist performing a senior's hip replacement.

Traditional Medicare has established demonstration projects to try and coordinate seniors' care, including several created by Obamacare. However, Medicare Advantage plans have under-taken such coordinated care for years—and largely succeeded at it. At a time when more and more seniors have joined Medicare Advantage, and when uncoordinated care helps keep health spending high, policy-makers should work to ensure that all seniors—and all Americans—have the coordinated care that Medicare Advantage provides.

But instead of allowing private plans to continue—whether for seniors enrolled in Medicare, or the under-65 population—single payer will make them "unlawful," and throw nearly 23 million seniors off their Medicare Advantage plans. All this so single-payer advocates can use the current Medicare program as a slush fund to *try* to finance government-run health care for all Americans, which has a terrible track record.

MEDICARE AS LIBERALS' BIG GOVERNMENT SLUSH FUND

Liquidating the current Medicare Trust Funds to finance a new single-payer program changes prior practices only in degree. President Obama's eponymous health-care law also raided Medicare to fund its new entitlements.

According to the Congressional Budget Office, Obamacare lowered Medicare spending by a total of $529 billion from 2010 through 2019.[24] (Some Republicans attacked these reductions as spending "cuts"; however, they did not reduce spending in absolute terms, but merely slowed Medicare's projected growth rates.) The law also increased Medicare payroll taxes by a total of $87 billion over the same period.[25]

The Obama administration and congressional Democrats attempted to use trust fund accounting to claim that these spending reductions could improve the solvency of the Part A (Hospital Insurance) Medicare Trust Fund by twelve years while supposedly funding the new coverage expansions under Obamacare. Asked at a House Energy and Commerce Committee hearing whether the provisions were being used to "save Medicare" or to "fund health care reform," Health and Human Services Secretary Kathleen Sebelius replied, "Both."[26]

The idea that one set of spending reductions could fund two programs at once defied not just common sense, but the analysis of non-partisan budget experts. The Congressional Budget Office called out this tactic as a budget gimmick:

---

24   Congressional Budget Office, Cost Estimate for H.R. 4872, Table 5.

25   Joint Committee on Taxation, "Estimated Revenue Effects of the Manager's Amendment to the Revenue Provisions Contained in the Patient Protection and Affordable Care Act, as Passed by the Senate on December 24, 2009," Publication JCX-10-10, March 11, 2010, https://www.jct.gov/publications.html?func=startdown&id=3663.

26   Testimony of Health and Human Services Secretary Kathleen Sebelius before the House Energy and Commerce Subcommittee on Health, March 3, 2011, video available at https://www.youtube.com/watch?v=ukaIZ7pmabo.

The savings to the [Medicare] trust fund under [Obamacare] would be received by the government only once, so they cannot be set aside to pay for future spending and, at the same time, pay for current spending….To describe the full amount of [Medicare] trust fund savings as both improving the government's ability to pay future Medicare benefits and financing new spending outside of Medicare would essentially double-count a large share of those savings and thus overstate the improvement in the government's fiscal position.[27]

The Medicare actuary agreed with CBO, writing that "in practice, the improved [Medicare] financing cannot be simultaneously used to finance other federal outlays (such as coverage expansions under [Obamacare]) and to extend the [life of the] trust fund, despite the appearance of this result from the respective accounting conventions."[28]

To put it another way: When Democrats used the Medicare savings on Obamacare's new entitlements, they did so at the opportunity cost of true entitlement reform. The Medicare program looked better on paper, but became worse in reality, because Obamacare spent money that could otherwise have gone toward improving the program's long-term solvency, or allowing Americans to control more of their own earnings.

---

27   Congressional Budget Office, "Effects of the Patient Protection and Affordable Care Act on the Federal Budget and the Balance in the Hospital Insurance Trust Fund," December 23, 2009, https://www.cbo.gov/publication/25017.

28   Solomon Mussey, "Estimated Effects of the Patient Protection and Affordable Care Act, as Amended, on the Year of Exhaustion for the Part A Trust Fund, Part B Premiums, and Part A and B Co-Insurance Amounts," Centers for Medicare and Medicaid Services Office of the Actuary memorandum, April 22, 2010, https://www.cms.gov/Research-Statistics-Data-and-Systems/Research/ActuarialStudies/Downloads/PPACA_Medicare_2010-04-22.pdf.

UNDERMINING THE PROMISE TO SENIORS

The single-payer bill would take the Obamacare gimmick one step further, by taking one program (the current Medicare entitlement) that already lacks funds and transferring it into another program with an *even larger* funding shortfall. Rather than working to fix Medicare's existing insolvency, the single-payer bills would instead undermine it. This would drop seniors into a new program with even more fragile funding.

The Medicare trustees report quantifies the current program's funding shortfalls. From 2019 through 2028, the Medicare actuary's office predicts that the program's Hospital Insurance (Part A) trust fund will take in $4.13 trillion in payroll tax and other revenue, while paying out $4.55 trillion in benefits.[29] The program's income does not meet expenses—a problem, to be sure, not least because the trustees project the trust fund will become exhausted (i.e., have a zero balance) by 2026. However, over the coming decade, estimated revenue can fund the lion's share—90.9%, to be exact—of the program's estimated expenses.

But what if you believe that the accounting gimmicks Obamacare exploited create an unrealistically rosy view of Medicare's finances? The Medicare trustees report issued in 2009, the last year before Obamacare's enactment, provides some sense of the program's solvency without relying on accounting gimmicks, albeit with older data.

That report indicated that, over the 25 years from 2009 through 2033, the Medicare trust fund would receive a total of 3.47% of the nation's taxable payroll in income, while paying out

---

29   Centers for Medicare and Medicaid Services, "2019 Trustees Report," Table III.
      B5, Estimated Operations of the HI Trust Fund during Calendar Years 2018-2028,
      under Alternative Sets of Assumptions, p. 57.

a total of 4.88% of taxable payroll in benefits.[30] Under this scenario, Medicare could fund only about two-thirds (3.47% divided by 4.88%, or 71.1%) of its estimated expenses through 2033.

Compare these two scenarios to a potential single-payer program, which both liberal and conservative organizations believe would cost well over $30 trillion. In 2016, the left-leaning Urban Institute published an analysis estimating federal spending would increase by $32 trillion between 2017 and 2026.[31] Two years later, the right-leaning Mercatus Center published a study estimating that federal spending under a single-payer plan would rise by $32.6 trillion from 2022 through 2031.[32] At a time when federal deficits are projected to approach $900 billion during the current fiscal year, and will total an estimated $11.4 trillion in the decade beyond, this proposed new spending would render our federal government's obligations utterly impossible, since they are already unsustainable.[33]

---

30   Centers for Medicare and Medicaid Services, "2009 Annual Report of the Boards of Trustees of the Federal Hospital Insurance and Federal Supplemental Medical Insurance Trust Funds," August 5, 2009, https://www.cms.gov/Research-Statistics-Data-and-Systems/Statistics-Trends-and-Reports/ReportsTrustFunds/Downloads/TR2009.pdf, Table III.B8, HI Actuarial Balances under Three Sets of Assumptions, p. 65.

31   John Holahan, *et al.*, "The Sanders Single Payer Health Care Plan: The Effect on National Health Expenditures and Federal and State Spending," Urban Institute, May 9, 2016, https://www.urban.org/sites/default/files/publication/80486/200785-The-Sanders-Single-Payer-Health-Care-Plan.pdf.

32   Charles Blahous, "The Costs of a National Single Payer Health Care System" Mercatus Center, July 30, 2018, https://www.mercatus.org/system/files/blahous-costs-medicare-mercatus-working-paper-v1_1.pdf.

33   Congressional Budget Office, May 2019 budget baseline, https://www.cbo.gov/system/files/2019-05/51118-2019-05-budgetprojections.xlsx, Table 1: CBO's Baseline Budget Projections, by Category.

In calculating the tax increases necessary to finance single-payer's increased spending, the Mercatus Center's study helpfully quantified the new program's under-funding. During the decade from 2022 through 2031, the study estimates that federal health expenditures under the single-payer program would total $54.6 trillion.[34] By comparison, the paper uses Congressional Budget Office estimates for federal spending on health care—net federal spending for Medicare, Medicaid, and Obamacare subsidies, along with the tax subsidies provided for employer-sponsored health insurance—to quantify the existing resources that the bill would re-purpose toward the new program.

That spending totals $21.9 trillion—or only 40.2% of the total estimated spending on the single-payer program.[35] As the Mercatus study also notes, current corporate and individual income tax rates would have to more than double to pay for all this proposed new spending, at a time when our nation already faces trillions of dollars in deficits to pay for existing government spending.

Moreover, the Mercatus Center study uses a series of assumptions very favorable to single-payer supporters.[36] The Mercatus study does not assume any increase in spending from "benefit tourism"—that is, individuals traveling to the United States, whether temporarily or permanently, to access "free" health care. However, it does assume that the new single-payer

---

34 Blahous, "The Costs," Table 2, Financial Effects of Medicare for All Act, in Billions of Dollars, p. 7.

35 Ibid.

36 Chris Jacobs, "Bernie Sanders Supporters Admit His Socialized Medicine Plan Will Ration Care," *The Federalist* August 2, 2018, http://thefederalist.com/2018/08/02/bernie-sanders-supporters-admit-socialized-medicine-plan-will-ration-care/.

program can 1) drive down drug costs by increasing usage of generic drugs, 2) generate significant savings through lower administrative costs, and 3) force both hospitals and doctors to accept lower, Medicare-level reimbursement rates.

If any of the Mercatus Center's very favorable assumptions about single payer prove incorrect, total spending on the new program would rise significantly. For instance, the Urban Institute's estimate included $2.9-$3.6 trillion in spending on long-term supports and services—services not included in the Mercatus study, but recently added to the single-payer bill.[37] Including this additional spending would raise the cost of the single-payer program even further—and worsen its under-funding.

To put it another way, the single-payer bill would transfer seniors from a Medicare program currently funded at between 71% (using unfavorable assumptions) and 91% (using favorable assumptions) of its expenses over the next 10-15 years, and place them in a new program with proposed funding of 40% (at best) of its obligations over the coming decade-plus. This would clearly make seniors' health care less secure.

PROBLEMATIC PRIORITIES

Some might find the above analysis pointless, for a variety of reasons: The studies in question use different time horizons; insolvency really only applies to one part of Medicare (Part A);

---

37 John Holahan and Linda Blumberg, "Estimating the Cost of a Single Payer Plan," Urban Institute, October 9, 2018, https://www.urban.org/sites/default/files/publication/99151/estimating_the_cost_of_a_single-payer_plan_0.pdf, p. 2. The $2.9 trillion estimate covers the 2017-2026 budget window in the original Urban study, while the higher $3.6 trillion number covers the (later) 2022-2031 budget window in the Mercatus paper.

and Democrats will propose tax increases to pay for the rest of the single-payer bill (maybe).[38] What's the point?

Ultimately, the question comes down to priorities. As with Obamacare a decade ago, the Left wants to use Medicare as a piggy bank to pay for yet another welfare state expansion. But that piggy bank is already coming up empty to pay for existing programs. Adding more recipients would only empty the piggy bank faster. As with the peanut butter on the proverbial slice of bread, spreading resources too thin will satisfy no one—and will only undermine everyone's security.

Surprisingly, one leading Democrat made an eloquent case for setting priorities opposite to the philosophy underpinning single payer. In September 2009, Rep. Steny Hoyer (D-MD)—then, as now, the House majority leader—rose in opposition to legislation designed to forestall a temporary Medicare premium increase for some seniors. In his speech, Hoyer explained that the majority of seniors who would benefit from the legislation had relatively high incomes. As a result, Hoyer concluded that, with deficits and debt rising, Congress had better priorities than to provide additional subsidies to the affluent:

> At some point in time, my friends, we have to buck up our courage and our judgement and say, *if we take care of everybody, we won't be able to take care of those who need us most.* That's my concern. If we take care of everybody, irrespective of their ability to pay for themselves, the Ross Perots of

---

38 Medicare Part A is funded largely by payroll taxes, and therefore has a more narrowly defined funding mechanism. By contrast, general revenues fund Medicare Parts B and D; their unlimited draw on the Treasury makes the insolvency of these specific programs a moot point, although the programs' ever-rising unfunded obligations weigh heavily on the federal budget.

America, frankly, the Steny Hoyers of America, then we will not be able to take care of those most in need in America. [Emphasis added.][39]

"If we take care of everybody, we won't be able to take care of those who need us most." Few politicians want to make such an admission. Some seem pathologically incapable of doing so. Most politicians run for office because they want to be liked; telling citizens "No" doesn't come naturally. Telling people "No" won't help politicians' re-election odds either.

But single payer takes saying "Yes" to impossibly absurd levels. Because the bill bans private insurance, most individuals will have to use the government-run system. And it will take Medicare dollars currently earmarked for seniors to subsidize this health coverage for the affluent.

Abolishing the current Medicare program to fund wealthy individuals' health care sounds like the kind of accusatory claim that a socialist like Sanders would level against Republicans. But in reality, his single-payer legislation would do just that. Sanders's socialist utopia would not only further jeopardize the security past generations expected of Medicare, it would also cost all taxpayers more than we can bear.

---

39   Floor Remarks of Rep. Steny Hoyer on H.R. 3631, Medicare Premium Fairness Act of 2009, *Congressional Record*, September 24, 2009, https://www.congress.gov/congressional-record/2009/09/24/house-section/article/H9908-1, pp. H9913-14.

3

THE $32 TRILLION QUESTION: HOW GOVERNMENT SPENDING WILL RISE

KEY POINTS

- Both liberal and conservative think-tanks have estimated that a single-payer program would increase federal spending by approximately $32 trillion over a decade.

- Federal spending would rise in part because provisions of the plan—eliminating cost-sharing, and a very expensive benefit package—would encourage individuals to consume more care than they need.

- Single payer would also extend health benefits to more people, including individuals unlawfully present in the

United States, and potential benefit tourists seeking to capitalize upon "free" health care funded by American taxpayers.

- Potential sources of savings, like reduced administrative costs, cannot offset the extra spending caused by additional demand for health care—unless the federal government sets provider payments very low, or otherwise restricts the available supply of care.

- Multiple data points indicate that recipients often do not value the government-provided health coverage they have now, suggesting that the enormous expense of a single-payer plan would not represent a good value for taxpayers' money.

The number seems almost too large to comprehend. $32 trillion—or, to be more precise, $32,000,000,000,000. That sum exceeds the United States' entire economic output in 2018 by about 40%, or roughly $12 trillion.[1] That means 40% more than all the goods and services all Americans, in the world's largest economy, produce in a year. Yet that number also represents the amount by which multiple studies estimate a single-payer program would increase national taxpayer spending over the course of a decade.[2]

---

1   Bureau of Economic Analysis, "Gross Domestic Product: Fourth Quarter 2018 and Annual 2018 (Third Estimate)," Report BEA 19-12, March 28, 2018, https://www.bea.gov/system/files/2019-03/gdp4q18_3rd_1.pdf, Table 3, Gross Domestic Product: Level and Change from Preceding Period, p. 9.

2   John Holahan, *et al.*, "The Sanders Single Payer Health Care Plan: The Effect on National Health Expenditures and Federal and State Spending," Urban Institute, May 9, 2016, https://www.urban.org/sites/default/files/publication/80486/200785-The-Sanders-Single-Payer-Health-Care-Plan.pdf; Charles Blahous, "The Costs of a National Single Payer Health Care System" Mercatus Center, July 30, 2018, https://www.mercatus.org/system/files/blahous-costs-medicare-mercatus-working-paper-v1_1.pdf.

Much remains uncertain about the fiscal effects of a move to single payer, although we know for certain it will be very expensive. In 2018, the Urban Institute released a follow-up paper just to explain the similarities and differences between their analysis and the Mercatus study.[3] Economists from across the political spectrum have offered a series of cost estimates for single payer, which reflect varying assumptions about the legislation and its effects.[4] But because the United States has never made such a large and wide-ranging change to its health markets—let alone the economy as a whole—its unprecedented nature by definition makes predicting all the precise effects extremely difficult.[5]

In May 2019, the Congressional Budget Office (CBO) weighed in with a report highlighting some of the decisions surrounding a move to single payer.[6] The study admitted that enacting such a system would represent "a major undertaking that would involve substantial changes in the sources and extent

3   John Holahan and Linda Blumberg, "Estimating the Cost of a Single Payer Plan" Urban Institute, October 9, 2018, https://www.urban.org/sites/default/files/publication/99151/estimating_the_cost_of_a_single-payer_plan_0.pdf.

4   Josh Katz, Kevin Quealy, and Margot Sanger-Katz, "Would 'Medicare for All' Save Billions or Cost Billions?" *New York Times,* April 10, 2019, https://www.nytimes.com/interactive/2019/04/10/upshot/medicare-for-all-bernie-sanders-cost-estimates.html.

5   Reed Abelson and Margot Sanger-Katz, "Medicare for All Would Abolish Private Insurance: 'There's No Precedent in American History,'" *New York Times,* March 23, 2019, https://www.nytimes.com/2019/03/23/health/private-health-insurance-medicare-for-all-bernie-sanders.html.

6   Congressional Budget Office, "Key Design Components and Considerations for Establishing a Single Payer Health Care System," May 1, 2019, https://www.cbo.gov/system/files/2019-05/55150-singlepayer.pdf.

of [health care] coverage," adding that "the transition toward a single-payer system could be complicated, challenging, and potentially disruptive."[7] However, the budget analysts largely couched their assessments in hypothetical language laying out various policy choices, using the word "would" 245 times and "could" 209 times in a 30-page document.[8]

Even though CBO has yet to release a specific cost estimate for the House and Senate single-payer bills, several elements of the legislative proposals include measures likely to increase spending on health care rather than reduce it. Providing more benefits to more people, and providing virtually all those benefits without requiring them to help pay for their care at the time of service, will induce additional demand for care. People will go to the doctor more often if other people will foot the bill. As a result, government will have to contain costs by lowering payments to doctors and hospitals, limiting the care available, or—more likely—some combination of both.

Moreover, this added spending may not deliver much additional benefit for patients. Under single payer, the federal government will fund all health services the government decides to provide for "free," but it will not fund other goods and services that patients consider of greater value, even those that might improve Americans' health.

To most Americans, the idea that Washington will spend approximately $32 trillion on a new health-care system sounds shocking enough. But if this tremendous growth in government

---

7   Ibid., pp. 1, 3.

8   Chris Jacobs, "The CBO Report on Single Payer Isn't the One We Deserve to See," *The Federalist* May 3, 2019, https://thefederalist.com/2019/05/03/cbo-report-single-payer-isnt-one-deserve-see/.

spending yields limited benefits, single payer becomes not just an idealistic obsession of the socialist left, but also a massively wasteful one.

INCREASING SPENDING BY INCREASING DEMAND

Imagine you won a shopping spree at a retail store. If you could run through the aisles, grab whatever you liked, and not have to pay for it, would you grab more clothes or goods than you need? Might you even take some things you didn't necessarily like, but felt that you could take because they were "free"? Most people would probably say yes.

Likewise, consider that staple of American cuisine, the all-you-can-eat buffet. Most people overeat at buffets, such that researchers have analyzed the deep-seated psychological urges in our brains that prompt us to over-consume food when it is plentiful.[9] Other people may simply feel the need to "get their money's worth" from their admission to the all-you-can-eat feast.

Some of the same forces would apply under a single-payer health care system. Because patients would face virtually no cost-sharing, they would have little incentive not to consume additional care. For instance, a patient with a mild cold who previously might have treated her symptoms with bed rest and over-the-counter remedies might instead decide to see the doctor "just to be safe," or because "I already paid for this health care through higher taxes, so why shouldn't I get my money's worth?"

Obviously, this analogy has its limits. Few rational individuals would subject themselves to invasive, and potentially

---

9   Gary Wenk, "Why Do We Overeat at the Buffet Table?" *Psychology Today,* October 4, 2010, https://www.psychologytoday.com/intl/blog/your-brain-food/201010/why-do-we-overeat-the-buffet-table.

painful or dangerous, medical procedures just to "get their money's worth" out of the health-care system. But making health care so easy to access would encourage additional spending. In fact, as we shall soon see, two analyses of single-payer health plans assumed that demand for health care would rise so quickly that the available supply could not meet it.

Both single-payer bills contain provisions that would cause people to use more health care. First, both effectively abolish cost-sharing for patients—deductibles, co-payments, co-insurance, and the like. The House bill would abolish cost-sharing completely, while the Senate legislation would permit very limited cost-sharing for prescription drugs: up to an annual maximum of $200 per person.[10]

Second, both pieces of legislation would prescribe a list of benefits more comprehensive than existing insurance plans. For instance, both bills would cover "oral health, audiology, and vision services," along with "necessary transportation to receive health care services" for those with disabilities or low-incomes.[11] Both bills would also include a pathway for the single-payer plan to cover treatments of "complementary and integrative medicine"—acupuncture and related alternative therapies—provided that the secretary of Health and Human Services and related experts consider them appropriate for the benefits package.[12]

By comparison, many employers do not provide these types of benefits outlined in the House and Senate single-payer bills.

---

10   Section 202(a) of H.R. 1384, the Medicare for All Act of 2019; Section 202(b) of S. 1129, the Medicare for All Act of 2019.

11   Section 201(a) of H.R. 1384; Section 201(a) of S. 1129.

12   Section 201(d) of H.R. 1384; Section 201(c) of S. 1129.

Only two-thirds (66%) of employers who offer health benefits to their employees also offer dental insurance, and fewer than half (49%) offer vision coverage.[13] Moreover, sizable percentages of employers that do offer dental and vision coverage do not contribute toward this insurance, such that fewer than one-third of employers subsidize vision coverage.[14] As a result, many Americans covered through employer-provided plans do not currently receive the types of subsidized supplemental benefits that the single-payer plan would cover.

Because the single-payer bills would provide patients additional benefits, and without cost-sharing, these changes will increase demand for care. For instance, in 2009 CBO concluded that the new insurance regulations included in Obamacare— requiring health plans to cover certain "essential health benefits" and so forth—would raise health spending by encouraging individuals to use these newly provided benefits. The budget office observed that the "increased use of medical care resulting from lower cost sharing" would raise health spending, and calculated that "induced increase" as raising individual health insurance premiums by approximately 10%.[15]

---

13   Kaiser Family Foundation and Health Research and Education Trust, *Employer Health Benefits: 2017 Annual Survey*, September 19, 2017, http://files.kff.org/ attachment/Report-Employer-Health-Benefits-Annual-Survey-2017, Figure 2-17, Among Firms Offering Health Benefits, Percentage of Firms That Offer Voluntary Benefits in Addition to the Health Plan, by Firm Size, Region, and Industry, p. 49.

14   Ibid., Figure 2-19, Among Firms Offering Health Benefits, Percentage of Firms that Offer Supplemental Insurance Benefits in Addition to Benefits Offered through the Health Plan, by Firm Size, p. 50.

15   Congressional Budget Office, Letter to Sen. Evan Bayh regarding health insurance premiums, November 30, 2009, https://www.cbo.gov/sites/default/files/111th-congress-2009-2010/reports/11-30-premiums.pdf, pp. 9-10.

Most analyses of single payer assume that the richer benefit package and virtual elimination of cost-sharing will increase demand for health care, but they vary on specific details. For instance, the Mercatus Center study concluded that eliminating cost-sharing will raise overall spending by 11%, while a Rand Corporation study cited an 8% rise in health spending due to this factor.[16] Remember, single-payer advocates tell you the opposite, that government-run health care will reduce costs. It's just not true.

NEW ENTITLEMENT WILL RAISE SPENDING

One particular provision in the single-payer bills will lead to a sizable increase in overall health spending. While prior iterations of single payer did not pay for long-term care supports and services, the bills introduced in 2019 now include these services, raising program spending.

The House and Senate versions of the legislation take slightly different approaches to providing long-term care benefits. The House bill would have taxpayers pay for such supports and services, whether provided in an institutional setting (i.e., a nursing home) or in a home-based setting; however, it requires that "unless an individual elects otherwise...recipients shall receive home and community-based" services.[17] By contrast, the Senate legislation only provides for coverage of home and community-based services through the federal program. Under the Senate bill, states would retain coverage of nursing home benefits through their existing Medicaid systems, but nursing

---

16   Katz, Quealy, and Sanger-Katz, "Would 'Medicare for All' Save Billions?"

17   Section 204 of H.R. 1384.

home residents would receive health-care benefits through the federal program.[18]

In both cases, however, the single-payer program will result in higher spending. Under current law, Medicare covers long-term care only in very limited circumstances. While state Medicaid programs do cover long-term supports and services, individuals must meet income and asset tests to qualify for coverage. Moreover, while state Medicaid programs *must* cover nursing home care as a mandatory benefit, they *may* cover home and community-based services as an optional benefit.[19]

Because individuals must meet asset and income tests to qualify for Medicaid coverage of long-term supports and services, and because most state Medicaid programs limit their coverage of home and community-based care, many individuals who might otherwise seek such services do not. Instead, unpaid care—whether from friends, relatives, or both—often serves as a substitute for formal, paid care.

Estimates suggest this unpaid care totaled $470 billion in 2013—more than the $366 billion in formal spending on such services as of 2016.[20] However, if a single-payer system pays for long-term supports and services, many households that rely

---

18 Sections 201(a)(13) and 204 of S. 1129.

19 MaryBeth Musumeci and Molly O'Malley Watts, "Key State Policy Choices about Medicaid Home and Community-Based Services," Kaiser Family Foundation, April 4, 2019, https://www.kff.org/report-section/key-state-policy-choices-about-medicaid-home-and-community-based-services-issue-brief/.

20 Susan Reinhard, *et al.*, "Valuing the Invaluable: 2015 Update," AARP Public Policy Institute, July 2015, https://www.aarp.org/content/dam/aarp/ppi/2015/valuing-the-invaluable-2015-update-new.pdf; Kirsten Colello, "Who Pays for Long-Term Services and Supports," Congressional Research Service Report IF10343, August 22, 2018, https://fas.org/sgp/crs/misc/IF10343.pdf.

solely on unpaid care now would likely use them.

This change means broader coverage for long-term care would raise health-care spending. The CBO report on single payer noted that broader coverage of home-based care would result in a "particularly large," and therefore costly, shift from unpaid and informal care to paid, formal care.[21] The Urban Institute estimated that covering long-term supports and services would cost approximately $3 trillion over a decade.[22] The Rand Corporation concluded that providing these services as a covered benefit would triple—lead to a 200% increase in—spending on formal home care, and a 10% increase in spending on nursing home care.[23]

Of course, the new government health plan could mitigate this rise in spending the way state Medicaid programs do now, by restricting access to benefits. Because states are not required to cover home and community-based services, they can—and many do—impose waiting lists for care. At present, more than 707,000 individuals with disabilities remain on Medicaid waiting lists for home and community-based services.[24] Those

---

21   Congressional Budget Office, "Key Design Components."

22   Urban estimated $2.9 trillion in costs over the original ten-year budget window it examined (2017-2026), and $3.6 trillion in costs over the later ten-year budget window included in the Mercatus study (2022-2031). Holahan and Blumberg, "Estimating the Cost," p. 2.

23   Jodi Liu and Christine Eibner, "National Health Spending Estimates Under Medicare for All," Rand Corporation, April 2019, https://www.rand.org/pubs/research_reports/RR3106.html.

24   Kaiser Family Foundation, "Waiting List Enrollment for Medicaid Section 1915(c) Home and Community-Based Services Waivers," April 2019, https://www.kff.org/health-reform/state-indicator/waiting-lists-for-hcbs-waivers/?currentTimeframe=0&sortModel=%7B%22colId%22:%22Location%22,%22sort%22:%22asc%22%7D.

on the waiting list include people like Lindsay Overman and her daughter Skylar:

> "She [Skylar] was born with a rare medical neurological condition called schizencephaly," Overman told [the Heritage Foundation].
>
> In the past three months Skylar's condition has worsened. Last month she had surgery to relieve pressure on her brain and her family is paying $400 per month just for transportation to and from a summer program. A Medicaid waiver would help with the costs that go along with at-home care for children with disabilities.
>
> Skylar remains #754 on the waiver waiting list.[25]

Arkansas, where the Overmans live, decided to expand Medicaid to the able-bodied, rather than to eliminate the waiting list for individuals with disabilities, like Skylar. Arkansas, and other states, have expanded Medicaid benefits to able-bodied adults, while individuals with disabilities remain on waiting lists. Obamacare encourages these skewed state priorities, because the law effectively discriminates against the most vulnerable in society.[26]

Since Obamacare took effect, at least 21,904 individuals with disabilities have died on waiting lists for care in states that

---

25   Jason Peterson, "Waiver Commitment Wavering," KATV, June 15, 2016, https://katv.com/community/7-on-your-side/waiver-commitment-wavering.

26   Chris Jacobs, "How Obamacare Undermines American Values: Penalizing Work, Citizenship, Marriage, and the Disabled," Heritage Foundation *Backgrounder No. 2862*, November 21, 2013, http://www.heritage.org/research/reports/2013/11/how-obamacare-undermines-american-values-penalizing-work-marriage-citizenship-and-the-disabled.

expanded Medicaid.[27] This chilling statistic provides a very tangible reminder that an insurance card does not equal access to care—and a potential precursor to the ways a single-payer health-care system will attempt to reduce skyrocketing health-care spending.

MORE RECIPIENTS RECEIVING NEW BENEFITS

The single-payer bills would not just prescribe more covered benefits and services; they would extend that coverage to more people. Section 102 of both the House and Senate bills makes the wide remit of the program clear:

> (a) IN GENERAL.—Every individual who is a resident of the United States is entitled to benefits for health care services under this Act. The Secretary shall promulgate a rule that provides criteria for determining residency for eligibility purposes under this Act.[28]

By making anyone "who is a resident of the United States" eligible for benefits, instead of anyone who is a *citizen*, both bills would extend "free" health care to the millions of individuals present unlawfully.

An unlikely source has expressed disagreement with this approach: Hillary Clinton. In September 1993, when testifying before Congress about the legislation her health-care task force had proposed, she said the following about taxpayers paying for services to individuals unlawfully present:

---

27   Nicholas Horton, "Waiting for Help: The Medicaid Waiting List Crisis," Foundation for Government Accountability, March 6, 2018, https://thefga.org/wp-content/uploads/2018/03/WAITING-FOR-HELP-The-Medicaid-Waiting-List-Crisis-07302018.pdf.

28   Section 102(a) of H.R. 1384 and S. 1129.

We do not think the comprehensive health care benefits should be extended to those who are undocumented workers and illegal aliens. We do not want to do anything to encourage more illegal immigration into this country. We know now that too many people come in for medical care, as it is. We certainly don't want them having the same benefits that American citizens are entitled to have.[29]

According to Mrs. Clinton's reasoning from 1993, single payer will increase health costs in the United States, and increase unlawful migration into the United States.

Yet, in a sign of how much liberals continue to move ever leftward, some single-payer supporters now believe that American taxpayers should fund benefits for those in this country unlawfully. Asked by CNN about the language above in the Senate single-payer bill, and whether she supports "giving universal health care, Medicare for all to people who are in this country illegally," presidential candidate Sen. Kamala Harris (D-CA) responded thusly:

Let me just be very clear about this. I am opposed to any policy that would deny in our country any human being from access to [*sic*] public safety, public education or public health, period.[30]

Ironically enough, as we have already seen, Harris supports taking away the current health benefits held by hundreds of

---

29   Testimony of Hillary Clinton before the House Energy and Commerce Committee, September 28, 1993, video available at https://youtu.be/WTVQQubdJ-w?t=44.

30   *State of the Union*, CNN, May 12, 2019, http://www.cnn.com/ TRANSCRIPTS/1905/12/sotu.01.html.

millions of American citizens.[31] Yet, based on her comments, she would gladly use American taxpayer dollars to pay for benefits to individuals in this country unlawfully—which, as Clinton noted in 1993, will only encourage further unlawful migration to our shores.

Moreover, single-payer could well lead to an influx of "benefit tourism," with people flocking to the United States to receive care. The same section of the House and Senate bills requires the secretary of Health and Human Services (HHS) to promulgate rules designed to prevent individuals from traveling for the "sole purpose of obtaining health care" from the single-payer system.[32] But the bill only prohibits individuals from traveling for the *sole purpose* of receiving "free" health care. It does not even prohibit individuals from traveling for the *primary purpose* of receiving "free" care.

Based on the plain text of the legislation, it appears HHS would have little legal justification for denying anyone in the world use of the U.S. government health-care system, so long as he or she claims to have some other purpose—say, visiting a tourist site or two—associated with his or her visit. As with the other provisions in the law, this language will only increase demand for, and taxpayer spending on, health-care goods and services. It also means that hard-working American taxpayers could wind up footing the bill for treatments provided to foreign guests traveling to our shores for "free" health care.

---

31   Chris Jacobs, "Kamala Harris Reveals That Medicare for All Involves Ending
      All Private Insurance," *The Federalist* January 31, 2019, http://thefederalist.
      com/2019/01/31/kamala-harris-reveals-medicare-means-ending-private-insurance/.

32   Section 102(b) of H.R. 1384 and Section 102(b)(2) of S. 1129.

SAVINGS SOURCES UNCERTAIN AT BEST

The fact that the broader benefits a single-payer system promises will likely drive up health spending yields one obvious question: Will other provisions in the legislation help contain costs? As with other elements of single payer, one cannot quantify the precise effects, but the available data provide some clear reasons for doubt.

The federal government could generate significant savings from lowering reimbursements to doctors and hospitals, but that would also generate serious costs. Provisions in the House and the Senate bills suggest that the new single-payer program would use current Medicare rates—far lower than rates paid by private insurance plans—to reimburse doctors and hospitals.[33] As we shall see in future chapters, these lower payment rates could cause doctors and hospitals to lay off millions of health-care workers, prompt physicians to retire early, and even discourage would-be doctors from ever joining the medical profession.

When Sanders congratulated the Mercatus Center for its July 2018 analysis, claiming the study proved single payer would reduce overall health spending, he implicitly embraced its assumption that single payer would do so by paying hospitals and doctors at Medicare levels.[34] However, such lower payment levels would significantly alter health-care markets, and could prove unsustainable. If a single-payer system instead had to pay doctors and hospitals using current reimbursement rates—in other words, it could not save money by paying providers Medicare rates for all patients—the Mercatus paper concluded this one change would

---

33 See for instance Section 612 of H.R. 1384 and Section 611 of S. 1129.

34 Sen. Bernie Sanders, July 30, 2018, https://twitter.com/SenSanders/status/1024074723385401344.

raise spending by $5.4 trillion over a decade, more than wiping out any supposed savings from single payer.[35]

Second, a single-payer system could achieve savings from lower pharmaceutical spending, either by lowering payments to drug companies outright, encouraging greater use of cheaper generic drugs, or a combination of the two. Yet arbitrarily lowering payments could limit future medical innovation by discouraging investment in the pharmaceutical industry. This payment strategy would potentially result in short-term gain, but long-term pain, for American patients.

As for generic pharmaceuticals, such drugs already comprise 87% of prescriptions dispensed by the current Medicare Part D program, making it difficult to increase generic adoption even further.[36] Moreover, because both single-payer bills virtually prohibit cost-sharing, the government would have few economic incentives at its disposal to do so.[37] Finally, because prescription drugs represented just 9.4% of total health-care spending in 2018, even a sizable reduction in drug spending would yield only a modest reduction in overall health costs.[38]

---

35   Blahous, "The Costs," pp. 12-13.

36   Estimate relates to outpatient drugs in Medicare Part D only, and does not reflect drugs administered in hospitals or physicians' offices. Medicare Payment Advisory Commission, *Report to the Congress: Medicare Payment Policy*, March 15, 2019, http://medpac.gov/docs/default-source/reports/mar19_medpac_entirereport_sec.pdf?sfvrsn=0, p. 402.

37   Section 201(a) of H.R. 1384; Section 201(a) of S. 1129.

38   Centers for Medicare and Medicaid Services Office of the Actuary, "National Health Expenditure Projections 2018-2027," https://www.cms.gov/Research-Statistics-Data-and-Systems/Statistics-Trends-and-Reports/NationalHealthExpendData/Downloads/Proj2018Tables.zip, Table 2, National Health Expenditure Amounts and Annual Percent Change by Type of Expenditure: Calendar Years 2011-2027.

Third, single payer could yield administrative savings for both doctors and the government, due to the simplicity of billing one government-run insurer rather than many payers. But just as health information technology has not yielded its promised savings—government edicts have left frustrated emergency room physicians making an average of 4,000 mouse clicks in a single shift—so too could the new regulations required by a single-payer program swamp any potential reduction in billing-related expenses.[39] In addition, the continued prevalence of fraud and improper payments within Medicare and Medicaid, as outlined later, suggests that lower administrative expenses for government-run health programs come with their own costly trade-offs.

Overall, many estimates suggest that, rather than lowering health spending, a single-payer system will instead increase it. For example:

- The Rand Corporation estimated spending would increase by a total of 1.8%. However, this estimate assumed a supply constraint equal to 50% of the new demand—in other words, people would seek care under the new system, but could not access it. In the absence of this supply constraint, Rand assumed that overall health spending would rise by nearly 10%.[40]

- The Urban Institute estimated that bringing most national health spending into the federal system would

39   Fred Schulte and Erika Fry, "Death by 1,000 Clicks: Where Electronic Health Records Went Wrong," *Fortune*, March 18, 2019, https://khn.org/news/death-by-a-thousand-clicks/.

40   Liu and Eibner, "National Health Spending Estimates."

raise overall spending by 16.6% over a ten-year period.[41] Like Rand, the Urban researchers assumed that "not all increased demand could be met because provider capacity would be insufficient."[42] The Urban analysts did not quantify spending increases absent supply constraints, but it would obviously exceed the 16.6% figure that assumed such constraints.

- As noted above, the Mercatus study yielded some modest savings—approximately a 3.4% reduction in health spending over the course of a decade—largely because it assumed that single-payer plan would pay providers at current Medicare rates. If that assumption, or any other highly favorable assumption included in the study, did not materialize, single payer would *raise* national health spending.[43]

On balance, then, it appears that the single-payer bills, in addition to costing taxpayers tens of trillions of dollars, would raise health spending in the aggregate by increasing demand for health services. Single payer could reduce health spending only if it held provider rates low enough or imposed other capacity restraints that would limit access to care.

---

41   Holahan, *et al.*, "The Sanders Plan," Table 1, The Sanders Plan: The Impact on National Health Expenditures and Federal Spending, 2017 and 2017-2026, p. 4.

42   Ibid., p. 8.

43   Chris Jacobs, "Bernie Sanders Supporters Admit His Socialized Medicine Plan Will Ration Care," *The Federalist* August 2, 2018, http://thefederalist.com/2018/08/02/bernie-sanders-supporters-admit-socialized-medicine-plan-will-ration-care/.

ADDED SPENDING, BUT NOT ADDED VALUE

Apart from whether a single-payer system will raise or lower health costs, policy-makers should consider an even more important question: Does the added federal expenditure represent a wise policy choice? Here again, the available evidence casts significant doubt that it does.

First, providing services free at the point of service encourages additional health spending, but that spending does not appear to generate additional improvements in health. The famous Rand Health Insurance Experiment, funded by the Department of Health and Human Services beginning in the 1970s, assigned patients to a series of health plans of varying designs. The study found that patients assigned to plans with higher cost-sharing reduced their health spending, but in general, that lower health spending "had no adverse effect on participants' health."[44]

This theory has self-evident limits, as at some point rising cost-sharing will deter patients from obtaining treatments beneficial to their health. But the single-payer bills would make virtually all health care "free," with not so much as even a $5 or $10 co-pay. It does not require a PhD in economics to recognize how these altered incentives could easily result in people using more health care than they need. The Rand Health Insurance Experiment demonstrates this increase in spending would also likely not improve Americans' health.

Second, many beneficiaries in government-run health

---

44   Robert Brook, *et al.*, "The Health Insurance Experiment: A Classic Rand Study Speaks to the Current Health Care Reform Debate," Rand Corporation Research Brief, 2006, https://www.rand.org/content/dam/rand/pubs/research_briefs/2006/RAND_RB9174.pdf.

plans do not appear to value their current coverage. A study of Medicaid released in 2015 found that participants derive an average of $0.20 and $0.40 for every added dollar spent on the program. Other entities—often hospitals treating otherwise-uninsured patients—received a far greater benefit from Medicaid than the beneficiaries themselves, making it a questionable use of scarce taxpayer resources.[45]

Similar evidence about the value of health coverage comes from Obamacare. In the case of Medicaid expansion, able-bodied adults have signed up at a far faster rate than government analysts expected. By the end of 2016, enrollment in 24 states that expanded Medicaid exceeded projections by an average of 110%—meaning enrollment more than doubled states' maximum predictions.[46] By contrast, as of the first quarter of 2019, only 11.4 million individuals had coverage on the Obamacare exchanges—fewer than half the 24 million enrollees the Congressional Budget Office (CBO) had projected for 2019 enrollment at the time of Obamacare's passage.[47]

---

45   Amy Finkelstein, Nathaniel Hendren, and Erzo Luttmer, "The Value of Medicaid: Interpreting Results from the Oregon Health Insurance Experiment," National Bureau of Economic Research Working Paper 21308, June 2015, https://www.nber.org/papers/w21308.pdf.

46   Jonathan Ingram and Nicholas Horton, "Obamacare Expansion Enrollment Is Shattering Projections," Foundation for Government Accountability, November 16, 2016, https://thefga.org/download/ObamaCare-Expansion-is-Shattering-Projections.PDF, p. 5.

47   Centers for Medicare and Medicaid Services, "Health Insurance Exchanges 2019 Open Enrollment Report," March 25, 2019, https://www.cms.gov/newsroom/fact-sheets/health-insurance-exchanges-2019-open-enrollment-report; Congressional Budget Office, Cost Estimate for H.R. 4872 (Final Health Care Legislation), March 20, 2010, https://www.cbo.gov/sites/default/files/111th-congress-2009-2010/costestimate/amendreconprop.pdf, Table 4, Estimated Effects of the Insurance Coverage Provisions of the Reconciliation Proposal Combined with H.R. 3590 as Passed by the Senate, p. 21.

Exchange data also suggest a strong correlation between insurance subsidy amounts and enrollment. For instance, one 2016 analysis indicated that four-fifths (81%) of eligible individuals with incomes below 150% of the federal poverty level ($38,625 for a family of four in 2019), who qualify for the richest premium subsidies and help with co-payments and deductibles, have signed up for coverage.[48] By contrast, a far smaller fraction (16%) of those with incomes between three and four times the poverty level, who qualify for much smaller premium subsidies and do not receive co-payment assistance, enrolled in an exchange plan.[49]

All the available evidence—higher-than-expected enrollment in Medicaid, lower-than-expected enrollment in the Obamacare exchanges, and a stratification in exchange enrollment by income level—suggests that beneficiaries do not particularly value health insurance, or at least do not particularly value the coverage options Obamacare has provided them. They will sign up for "free" Medicaid coverage, which in most cases charges no premiums, deductibles, or co-payments, and they will sign up for heavily subsidized exchange plans. But when faced with out-of-pocket premium costs of more than $50-$100 per month, many seem content to forgo insurance.

This evidence raises obvious questions: Why should the federal government spend the tens of trillions of dollars that

48   Avalere Health, "The State of Exchanges: A Review of Trends and Opportunities to Grow and Stabilize the Market," Report for Aetna, October 2016, http://go.avalere. com/acton/attachment/12909/f-0352/1/-/-/-/-/20161005_Avalere_State%20of%20 Exchanges_Final_.pdf, Figure 3, Percent of Potential Exchange Population Making Marketplace Plan Selections in 2016, by Income, p. 6.

49   Ibid.

single-payer advocates propose to deliver something that many individuals of modest means appear not to value? The study of Medicaid spending that concluded recipients do not highly value their benefits noted how its results provided important evidence "for assessing the social value of providing Medicaid to low-income adults relative to alternative redistributive policies."[50]

For instance, what if a state offered Medicaid recipients who agreed to forgo Medicaid an alternative cash benefit equal to 50 cents of every dollar that the state would have spent on their coverage? Because the average beneficiary in the 2015 study valued his health benefit at only 20-40 cents, the beneficiary would receive a more highly valued benefit, and state taxpayers would reduce their overall spending on Medicaid.[51] Moreover, the beneficiary could spend the new dollars in ways that could improve his or her health—for instance, to rent an apartment in a safer neighborhood, or buy a car to commute to a higher-earning job.

Rather than reassessing our current safety net in light of the available evidence, however, single-payer supporters instead wish to place an even larger bet on services that many recipients and voters do not appear to value. This action reveals a sense of paternalism—the federal government and intellectual elites telling Americans what's best for them.[52]

This patronizing mentality also means single-payer will

50 Finkelstein, Hendren, and Luttmer, "The Value of Medicaid Spending," p. 1.

51 Chris Jacobs, "Medicaid vs. Cash for the Poor," *Wall Street Journal Think Tank* blog, June 18, 2015, https://blogs.wsj.com/washwire/2015/06/18/medicaid-vs-cash-for-poor/.

52 Megan McArdle, "Would the Poor Prefer Cash Instead of Medicaid?" *Bloomberg* June 10, 2015, https://www.bloomberg.com/opinion/articles/2015-06-10/would-the-poor-prefer-cash-instead-of-medicaid-.

not achieve good value for taxpayers' money. For instance, fewer than 1% of exchange enrollees purchased a platinum health plan—the plan with the richest benefits, and the lowest cost-sharing—as of the first quarter of 2019.[53] In 36 states, no insurers even bothered to offer these plans, because so few individuals wanted to buy them.[54]

So why should the federal government spend $32 trillion to give the American people the type of health coverage that millions of Americans have decided *not* to buy with their own money? The question should answer itself.

"FREE"—BUT COSTLY—CARE

Several years ago, the humorist P. J. O'Rourke quipped that "If you think health care is expensive now, wait until you see what it costs when it's free." Single payer epitomizes this quote, on several levels. First, providing health care to more people, and without asking them to pitch in even a token amount for it, would encourage additional demand for care. But as the Rand and Urban Institute studies concluded, the available supply of care could not meet that demand, likely leading to care rationing.

Second, every dollar federal taxpayers spend on health care brings opportunity costs. That means a tax dollar spent

---

53   CMS, "2019 Open Enrollment Report."

54   Admittedly, certain low-income individuals receive greater cost-sharing reductions, provided by insurers under the Obamacare statute, if they sign up for silver plans. However, the fact that insurers have failed even to offer platinum plans in most states suggests a decided lack of interest in these rich benefit packages. Centers for Medicare and Medicaid Services, 2019 Marketplace Open Enrollment State Level Public Use File, March 25, 2019, https://www.cms.gov/Research-Statistics-Data-and-Systems/Statistics-Trends-and-Reports/Marketplace-Products/Downloads/2019 OEPStateLevelPublicUseFile.zip.

on single payer is a tax dollar spent on some other voter priority, or returned to taxpayers for them to spend themselves. Individuals may indeed obtain some benefit from such spending, just like individuals obtain some benefit from Medicaid. But the federal government cannot assure that the dollars spent on single payer constitute what the American people consider the *highest and best* use of those resources. Only individual Americans making individual decisions about where to spend their own money can do that.

Third, the taxes necessary to fund the first decade's $32 trillion (or thereabouts) in new government spending would sap the economy of its vitality, permanently reducing its potential. In both the short and the long term, this cost to American society might prove the most damaging of all.

4

HOW SINGLE PAYER WILL SHOCK THE ECONOMY

KEY POINTS

- Single payer would profoundly damage the American economy, both inside and outside health care.

- By abolishing private health insurance, single payer could put more than 540,000 insurance industry employees out of work.

- Lower payment levels to hospitals under single payer could result in up to 1.5 million job losses, and potentially many more layoffs in physician offices and other health-care enterprises.

- Abolishing for-profit medical providers, as the House bill proposes, would eradicate hundreds of billions of dollars in companies' market capitalization, slashing the value of Americans' retirement accounts.

- If paid for by tax increases, single payer could make 71% of American households, and 85% of low-income households, worse off, even after accounting for the elimination of premiums, co-payments, and deductibles.

- Socialized medicine would raise taxes so high that Sen. Bernie Sanders's home state of Vermont had to shelve its plans for single-payer health care, after estimates suggested the plan would have required a 9.5% increase in income taxes, *plus* an 11.5% increase in payroll taxes.

- The tax increases required to fund single payer would reduce the non-health share of the economy by 19%, making the average household $17,000 per year poorer.

- The "transition fund" for worker retraining included in the single-payer bills does not even begin to outweigh all the negative effects the plan would bring to the American economy in both the short and the long term.

At the time of this writing, the United States stands on the cusp of the longest economic expansion in its history—a period of uninterrupted growth spanning more than a decade and presidents of both parties.[1] Enacting single-payer legislation could change all that.

---

[1]   Chris Isidore, "Where the Current Economic Boom Ranks in American History," CNN, January 30, 2018, https://money.cnn.com/2018/01/30/news/economy/us-economy-boom-history/index.html.

By reshuffling the entire health-care market, passing a single-payer law would shock one of the largest sectors of the American economy. The repercussions of such a major economic change could lead to a recession, a prolonged period of sluggish growth, or both.

As of 2017, Americans spent 17.9% of the U.S. gross domestic product on health care, a percentage projected to rise to 19.4% of GDP by 2027.[2] The United States spends more on health care than other industrialized nations do, both per person and as a percentage of gross domestic product.[3]

Some have argued that the United States needs to lower its level of health spending, or at minimum slow its growth. Policy makers often express their desire to "bend the cost curve," such that health-care spending will not continue to grow faster than inflation, or the economy as a whole.

However, a single-payer system represents exactly the wrong approach to lower health care costs, for multiple reasons, including these:

1. It does not focus on getting incentives right—if anything, it does just the opposite. As we have seen, by making health care "free," single payer will only *increase* demand for care. Having raised demand for health care significantly, single payer attempts to control spending by

----

2   Centers for Medicare and Medicaid Services Office of the Actuary, "National Health Expenditure Projections 2018-2027: Forecast Summary," February 20, 2019, https://www.cms.gov/Research-Statistics-Data-and-Systems/Statistics-Trends-and-Reports/NationalHealthExpendData/Downloads/ForecastSummary.pdf.

3   Organization for Economic Cooperation and Development, *Health at a Glance 2017: OECD Indicators*, February 2018, http://dx.doi.org/10.1787/health_glance-2017-en, chap. 7, "Health Expenditures," pp. 131-45.

limiting the available supply—restricting access to care through government rationing.

2. Government cannot allocate resources as efficiently as individuals can. Single-payer advocates foolishly assume that a group of bureaucrats can operate health markets better than individual doctors, patients, and hospitals can. Economic theory, to say nothing of sheer common sense, suggests the opposite.

3. A rapid transition from the current system to single payer—four years in the Senate bill, and a mere two years in the House bill—would lead to economic shocks. The legislation would put many individuals in the private health insurance industry out of business, and would sharply reduce payments to doctors and hospitals. Even if one believes the United States should reduce its level of health spending *over time*, doing so this quickly would almost guarantee a recession, given health care's share of the American economy.

4. The massive tax increases needed to fund single payer—more than doubling current individual and corporate income tax rates—would distort the economy even more, particularly if phased in rapidly as the new program comes online.[4]

Not only would single payer not lower health costs effectively; it would bring numerous adverse consequences, both

---

4   Charles Blahous, "The Costs of a National Single Payer Health Care System" Mercatus Center, July 30, 2018, https://www.mercatus.org/system/files/blahous-costs-medicare-mercatus-working-paper-v1_1.pdf.

within and outside the health sector. If enacted, the legislation would have negative effects that would ripple through the economy for many years to come.

ABOLISHING A MAJOR INDUSTRY

First and most obviously, single payer would make private health insurance "unlawful," effectively abolishing an entire industry. The *New York Times* noted that the legislation would unleash economic disruption on a scale never before seen in American history:

> The private health insurance business employs at least a half a million people, covers about 250 million Americans, and generates roughly a trillion dollars in revenues. Its companies' stocks are a staple of the mutual funds that make up millions of Americans' retirement savings.[5]

Many health insurance companies do have other lines of business. For instance, insurer Aetna was recently acquired by pharmacy behemoth CVS. And some individuals currently working for insurers could end up working for the single-payer program, particularly because the federal government would need to build an alternative insurance infrastructure very quickly.[6] But with health and medical insurance carriers employing 542,300 workers as of March 2019, a minimum of hundreds of thousands of Americans would face job disruption,

---

5   Reed Abelson and Margot Sanger-Katz, "Medicare for All Would Abolish Private Insurance: 'There's No Precedent in American History,'" *The New York Times* March 23, 2019, https://www.nytimes.com/2019/03/23/health/private-health-insurance-medicare-for-all-bernie-sanders.html.

6   Ibid.

if not outright unemployment, under single payer.[7]

Even talk of single-payer legislation has spooked investors in the health-care sector. On the day in February 2019 that Rep. Pramila Jayapal reintroduced her single-payer bill in the House, insurance industry stocks fell by nearly 5%.[8] The sell-off continued throughout the beginning of 2019, such that health-care stocks have shown one of the widest divergences from the broader Standard and Poor's 500 index—falling by 0.9%, even as the rest of the market gained a whopping 16%—this century.[9]

In response to news of the stock declines, Jayapal tweeted, "Sorry not sorry."[10] But the hundreds of thousands of American workers employed by health insurers, to say nothing of the millions of Americans with investments in the industry, might take a slightly less lackadaisical view toward massive disruption in their jobs, investments, and livelihoods.

LOWER REIMBURSEMENTS, FEWER JOBS

In addition to its direct effects on the insurance industry, single payer will attempt to save money by paying doctors and hospitals less. The legislation would base reimbursements on the

7   Bureau of Labor Statistics, "Employment, Hours, and Earnings from the Current Employment Statistics Survey: Direct Health and Medical Insurance Carriers," May 12, 2019, https://data.bls.gov/timeseries/CES5552411401.

8   Tatiana Darie, "Health Insurers Sink as 'Medicare for All' Idea Gains Traction," *Bloomberg,* February 27, 2019, https://www.bloomberg.com/news/articles/2019-02-27/health-insurers-sink-as-medicare-for-all-idea-gains-traction.

9   Amrith Ramkumar, "Health Care Stock Rout Deepens Amid Political Pressure," *Wall Street Journal,* April 17, 2019, https://www.wsj.com/articles/health-care-stock-rout-deepens-amid-political-pressure-11555516882.

10   Rep. Pramila Jayapal, February 27, 2019, https://twitter.com/RepJayapal/status/1100911532882477056.

current Medicare program, which pays doctors 75% of private insurance rates, and hospitals 60% of private insurance.[11] Medicare does not just pay doctors and hospitals less than private insurance—in many cases, it pays doctors and hospitals less than the cost of care. According to the Medicare actuary, 72% of hospitals lost money on their Medicare patients in 2017.[12]

Paying doctors and hospitals at much lower Medicare rates will lead to dramatic changes for the entire health-care sector. As the *New York Times* noted, job losses could represent the least of hospitals' concerns:

> Some hospitals, especially struggling rural centers, would close virtually overnight, according to policy experts. Others, they say, would try to offset the steep [reimbursement] cuts by laying off hundreds of thousands of workers and abandoning lower-paying services like mental health.[13]

11　See for instance Section 612(b) of H.R. 1384 and Section 611 of S. 1129, the Medicare for All Act of 2019. John Shatto and Kent Clemens, "Projected Medicare Expenditures under an Illustrative Scenario with Alternative Payment Updates to Medicare Providers," Centers for Medicare and Medicaid Services Office of the Actuary memorandum, April 22, 2019, https://www.cms.gov/Research-Statistics-Data-and-Systems/Statistics-Trends-and-Reports/ReportsTrustFunds/Downloads/2019TRAlternativeScenario.pdf.

12　Stephen Heffler, *et al.*, "Simulations of Affordable Care Act Medicare Payment Update Provisions on Part A Provider Margins," Centers for Medicare and Medicaid Services Office of the Actuary memorandum, April 22, 2019, https://www.cms.gov/Research-Statistics-Data-and-Systems/Statistics-Trends-and-Reports/ReportsTrustFunds/Downloads/ACAmarginsimulations2019.pdf.

13　Reed Abelson, "Hospitals Stand to Lose Billions under 'Medicare for All,'" *New York Times,* April 21, 2019, https://www.nytimes.com/2019/04/21/health/medicare-for-all-hospitals.html.

One health policy professor the *Times* interviewed admitted that "I have no idea what would happen" should a single-payer system apply lower reimbursements to all hospital patients.[14] But, should the Left succeed in forcing hospitals to become guinea pigs in this socialist experiment, one can credibly guess the likely outcome. As with many other elements of single payer, this change would hit the most vulnerable elements of the system—rural hospitals already struggling to make ends meet, or important yet unprofitable services and facilities—hardest.

To illustrate the impact of a single-payer system, the consulting firm Navigant outlined its effects on a hypothetical small hospital system, one with five hospitals, 1,000 total beds, and annual revenues of $1.2 billion. Navigant concluded that a single-payer system paying hospitals current Medicare rates would reduce the hospital network's revenue by $330 million—approximately one-quarter—turning a slight annual surplus (2.3%) into a massive operating loss (22.1%).[15] Obviously, a hospital couldn't long survive under conditions like that.

Another study showed the sizable impact of these reimbursement reductions on hospitals and jobs within hospitals nationwide. This analysis, published in the prestigious *Journal of the American Medical Association (JAMA)*, indicated a slightly smaller effect per hospital—an average 15.9% decline in revenue,

---

14   Ibid.

15   Jeff Goldsmith, Jeff Leibach, and Kurt Eicher, "Medicare Expansion: A Preliminary Analysis of Hospital Financial Impacts," Navigant Consulting, March 2019, https://www.navigant.com/-/media/www/site/insights/healthcare/2019/medicare-expansion-analysis.pdf.

as opposed to the one-quarter decline predicted by Navigant.[16]

However, the *JAMA* authors concluded that single payer would reduce hospital payments by $151 billion per year nationwide.[17] They noted that "an estimated 1.5 million hospital clinical and administrative jobs could be lost if hospitals reduced labor costs to compensate for the entire clinical shortfall;" if hospitals were willing to absorb some of the losses by eating into their operating margins, job losses could total "only" 855,999 workers.[18]

Several figures put the size and scale of the losses contemplated by single payer into perspective:

1. The Commerce Department's Bureau of Economic Analysis calculated total GDP for 2018 as $20.5 trillion.[19] A $151 billion reduction in hospital revenue equates to a reduction of approximately 0.7% of America's GDP—enough to turn a period of robust growth into sluggish growth, or to tip a period of sluggish growth into recession.

---

16 Kevin Schulman and Arnold Milstein, "The Implications of 'Medicare for All' for U.S. Hospitals," *Journal of the American Medical Association*, April 4, 2019, https://jamanetwork.com/journals/jama/fullarticle/2730485.

17 Ibid.

18 Ibid.

19 Bureau of Economic Analysis, "Gross Domestic Product: Fourth Quarter 2018 and Annual 2018 (Third Estimate)," Report BEA 19-12, March 28, 2019, https://www.bea.gov/system/files/2019-03/gdp4q18_3rd_1.pdf, Table 3, Gross Domestic Product: Level and Change from Preceding Period, p. 9.

2. In 2018, the United States created a total of just fewer than 2.7 million jobs.[20] Reductions in hospital employment on the magnitude outlined in the *JAMA* study would erase between one-third and one-half of that job growth.

3. As of 2018, spending on hospital care ($1.19 trillion) equaled less than one-third (32.7%) of total health spending of $3.65 trillion.[21] Extending the 15-25% payment reductions projected for the hospital sector to physician care ($728 billion in spending in 2018) and other sectors of health care will only magnify the effects on the broader economy.

The evidence strongly suggests that payment reductions on the magnitude single payer contemplates could result in millions of job losses, over and above those associated with eradicating the private insurance sector, and lead the economy into a recession.

ANNIHILATING WEALTH FOR THE MIDDLE CLASS

In addition to destroying the private insurance industry, the House's version of single payer will also disrupt the business models of many other health-care companies. While the Senate

---

20   Bureau of Labor Statistics, "The Employment Situation—March 2019," April 5, 2019, https://www.bls.gov/news.release/archives/empsit_04052019.pdf.

21   Centers for Medicare and Medicaid Services Office of the Actuary, "National Health Expenditure Projections," February 20, 2019, https://www.cms. gov/Research-Statistics-Data-and-Systems/Statistics-Trends-and-Reports/ NationalHealthExpendData/Downloads/Proj2018Tables.zip, Table 2, National Health Expenditure Amounts and Annual Percent Change by Type of Expenditure: Calendar Years 2011-2027.

bill does not include this provision, Section 614(b) of the House legislation specifically states that "payments to providers…may not take into account…or be used by a provider for…the profit or net revenue of the provider, or increasing the profit or net revenue of the provider."[22] In other words, if the House bill passes, every for-profit hospital, hospice, nursing home, home care agency, and other medical provider will immediately have to convert to not-for-profit status to participate in the single-payer plan.

Single-payer advocates would no doubt cheer the abolition of for-profit health care providers. The House bill also includes "Sense of Congress" language discussing the "moral imperative… to eliminate profit from the provision of health care."[23] But millions of Americans may not appreciate having untold amounts of wealth—much of which has accumulated in their 401(k)s, IRAs, and other investment and retirement vehicles—eradicated instantaneously to satisfy someone else's "moral imperative."

Health-care companies have created tremendous wealth for their shareholders, but a single-payer bill would eliminate much, if not all, of that wealth in a stroke. At the end of the first quarter of 2018, the largest health insurers had a combined market capitalization of $428.5 billion, according to the *Fortune* 500.[24] On top of these health insurers—whose main businesses would largely evaporate under both the House and Senate single-payer

---

22   Section 614(b) of H.R. 1384.

23   Section 614(a) of H.R. 1384.

24   Total includes the market capitalization of UnitedHealthGroup ($207.1 billion), Anthem ($56.2 billion), Aetna ($55.2 billion), Humana ($37.1 billion), Centene ($18.7 billion), Cigna ($40.7 billion), Molina Health Care ($4.9 billion), and WellCare Health Plans ($8.6 billion). Figures accurate as of March 29, 2018. See "Fortune 500," *Fortune*, http://fortune.com/fortune500/.

bills—many other health-care companies would have to convert to not-for-profit status under the House legislation, making their stockholders' shares worthless:

- HCA Health Care: Market capitalization of $34.2 billion

- Tenet Health Care: $2.5 billion

- Community Health Systems: $454 million

- DaVita: $12 billion

- Universal Health Services: $11.1 billion

- LifePoint Health: $1.8 billion

- Kindred Health Care: $836 million[25]

When coupled with the losses from for-profit insurers outlined above, the House version of single payer would likely eradicate at least *half a trillion dollars* in stock market value from various health care-related companies, whether health insurers or for-profit medical providers.

With a majority of all Americans (54%)—and a majority (54%) of Americans with modest incomes ($30,000-$75,000)—owning stocks, either directly or indirectly through mutual funds and retirement accounts, this sudden evaporation of wealth will affect the entire economy, not just "the rich" or speculators on Wall Street.[26] Besides destabilizing their retirements and futures, widespread stock market declines could lead to a negative "wealth

---

25   Ibid.

26   Jeffery M. Jones, "U.S. Stock Ownership Down Among All but Older, Higher-Income," Gallup, May 24, 2017, https://news.gallup.com/poll/211052/stock-ownership-down-among-older-higher-income.aspx.

effect," in which Americans spend less because they see their investments and retirement accounts shrinking.

TAXES—AND DEFICITS—WILL RISE

Apart from single payer's impact on the health-care sector specifically, the legislation would also affect other areas of the economy. While the House bill includes no means to fund the tens of trillions in new spending, Sen. Bernie Sanders released a white paper discussing funding options along with his legislation.[27] That white paper proposes a series of tax increases—some exclusively on "the rich," but many on the middle class as well:

1. "Creating a 4 percent income-based premium paid by employees, exempting the first $29,000 in income for a family of four";

2. "Imposing a 7.5 percent income-based premium paid by employers, exempting the first $2 million in payroll to protect small businesses";

3. "Eliminating health tax expenditures," such as the current exclusion from income and payroll taxes provided to employer-provided health insurance;

4. "Making the federal income tax more progressive, including a marginal tax rate of up to 70 percent on those making above $10 million, taxing earned and unearned income at the same rates, and limiting tax deductions for filers in the top tax bracket";

---

27 Sen. Bernie Sanders, "Financing Medicare for All," April 10, 2019, https://www. sanders.senate.gov/download/medicare-for-all-2019-financing?id=860FD1B9-3E8A-4ADD-8C1F-0DEDC8D45BC1&download=1&inline=file.

5. "Making the estate tax more progressive, including a 77 percent top rate on an inheritance above $1 billion";

6. "Establishing a tax on extreme wealth," a term Sanders chose not to define specifically;

7. "Closing the 'Gingrich-Edwards Loophole,'" which refers to individuals who set up corporations to reduce their payroll tax liability;

8. "Imposing a fee on large financial institutions"; and

9. "Repealing corporate accounting gimmicks."[28]

These proposals track closely with the 2013 version of Sanders's single-payer legislation. That bill contained four explicit tax increases:

1. A 6.7% increase in the payroll tax on employers;

2. An income tax increase of 2.2% on taxable income below $200,000 for an individual and $250,000 for a family, rising to a maximum of 5.2% for individual and family income over $600,000, with the thresholds adjusted for inflation;

3. An additional 5.4% surcharge on adjusted gross income over $500,000 for an individual and $1,000,000 for a family, with these thresholds *not* adjusted for inflation; and

---

28   Ibid.; Mark Koba, "How the Gingrich-Edwards Tax Loophole Works," CNBC, March 5, 2014, https://www.cnbc.com/2014/03/05/cnbc-explains-the-gingrich-edwards-tax-loophole.html.

4. A 0.02% tax on stock and other financial market trans-
actions, with a credit of $250 per individual ($500 for a
joint return) designed to offset the effects of the tax for
middle-income households.[29]

Unfortunately, however, Sanders's proposed tax increases
carry two major problems. First, it appears unlikely that even
these tax increases will pay for the entire cost of his proposed
system. Emory University economist Kenneth Thorpe analyzed
a prior version of Sanders's plan during the 2016 campaign,
and concluded that the tax increases did not come close to fully
paying for the cost of his proposed new spending:

> The average annual cost of the plan would be approximately
> $2.5 trillion per year creating an average of over a $1 trillion
> per year financing shortfall. To fund the program, payroll and
> income taxes would have to increase from a combined 8.4
> percent in the Sanders plan to 20 percent while also retaining
> all remaining tax increases on capital gains, increased marginal
> tax rates, the estate tax, and eliminating tax expenditures.[30]

Admittedly, Sanders's plan has changed since Thorpe's 2016
analysis. When releasing his 2019 single-payer bill, Sanders
proposed greater payroll tax increases (7.5% versus 6.7%) and
income tax increases (4% versus 2.2%) than his 2013 legislation.
However, Sanders has also proposed even more spending in the
updated single-payer bill.

As the last chapter noted, the 2019 version of single payer

---

29   Title VIII of S. 1782 (113th Congress), the American Health Security Act of 2013.

30   Kenneth Thorpe, "An Analysis of Sen. Sanders's Single Payer Plan," January 27,
      2016, https://www.healthcare-now.org/296831690-Kenneth-Thorpe-s-analysis-of-
      Bernie-Sanders-s-single-payer-proposal.pdf, p. 1.

would also cover long-term supports and services—an addition that could raise government spending by approximately $3 trillion over a decade.[31] It therefore remains unlikely that, despite the greater tax increases Sanders outlined in 2019, these tax hikes would come close to paying for all the new spending he has proposed.

BETTER OR WORSE OFF?

More to the point, would those tax increases be "worth it" to the average American? To put it another way, would people pay more or less under single payer than they do under the status quo? At an April 2019 town hall, Sanders claimed that "the overwhelming majority of people are going to end up paying less for health care because they're not paying premiums, co-payments, and deductibles."[32]

But a *Bloomberg* article notes the inherent problem with these types of claims: almost by definition, a single-payer plan would have to raise taxes on lower and middle-income families:

> To pay for [expensive government] programs, [2020 presidential candidates] have focused on taxing the rich. But many of the plans they've put on the table would require across-the-board tax increases that would hit middle-earners as well as the wealthy, public policy analysts say. None more than [single payer.]

---

31   John Holahan and Linda Blumberg, "Estimating the Cost of a Single Payer Plan," Urban Institute, October 9, 2018, https://www.urban.org/sites/default/files/publication/99151/estimating_the_cost_of_a_single-payer_plan_0.pdf, p. 2 (see chap. 2, n. 37).

32   Tami Luhby, "Can Taxing the Rich Pay for Bernie Sanders's Medicare for All Plan?" CNN April 16, 2019, https://www.cnn.com/2019/04/16/politics/medicare-for-all-rich-taxes/index.html.

Raising the more than $30 trillion needed to fund Sanders's health plan over a decade would require doubling all personal and corporate income taxes or tripling payroll taxes, which are split between employees and employers, said Marc Goldwein, a senior vice president at the non-partisan Committee for a Responsible Federal Budget.

"There's a lot of money out there, but there isn't $30 trillion sitting around from high earners," he said. "It just doesn't exist."[33]

The *Bloomberg* article noted that the list of tax increases Sanders has outlined to pay for his proposal to date would cover only about half its estimated costs. Moreover, a tripling of the payroll tax would cause the average family's tax bills to increase significantly.[34]

The sole analysis that attempted to quantify winners and losers under the Sanders plan found his claim wanting, and that most people would pay *more* under single payer. In his 2016 analysis, Thorpe also concluded that, if fully paid for via income and payroll tax increases, the Sanders plan would leave nearly three-quarters (71%) of American households worse off financially than the status quo—even after accounting for the elimination of health insurance premiums and cost-sharing under the plan.[35]

---

33   Laura Davison, "Tax Hikes on the Wealthy Alone Can't Pay for 'Medicare for All,'" *Bloomberg,* May 9, 2019, https://www.bloomberg.com/news/articles/2019-05-09/tax-hikes-on-wealthy-alone-can-t-pay-for-medicare-for-all-plan.

34   Ibid.

35   Thorpe, "An Analysis," Table 3, Number of Health Insurance Units Paying More and Less for Health Care Under Single Payer Compared to Current Law When Plan Is Fully Financed, p. 5.

Worse yet, according to Thorpe: "Some 85 percent of low income working populations on Medicaid would also pay more in taxes and reduced wage growth compared to any additional single payer benefits" if Sanders funded his plan through tax increases.[36] In other words, single payer would in yet another way most harm the vulnerable patients that Sanders claims it would help.

Moreover, Sanders's claim about millions of Americans saving money through single payer defies common sense. As one researcher from the liberal Urban Institute noted:

> We should always be suspect of any public policy—especially when it comes to something as complicated as health care— when anybody tells us everybody is going to get more and pay less for it. It's really not possible.[37]

We've seen these types of claims before, of course. Barack Obama famously pledged dozens of times that "If you like your plan, you can keep it."[38] He also claimed that his health plan would lower Americans' health insurance premiums—not merely slow the rate of increase, mind you, but reduce them in absolute terms—by an average of $2,500 per family per year.[39] He also

---

36 Ibid.

37 Paige Winfield Cunningham, "The Health 202: Bernie Sanders Says Medicare for All Would Reduce Health Spending, But That's Unclear," *Washington Post* April 17, 2019, https://www.washingtonpost.com/news/powerpost/paloma/the-health-202/2019/04/17/the-health-202-bernie-sanders-says-medicare-for-all-would-reduce-health-spending-but-that-s-unclear/5cb60483a7a0a475985bd484/.

38 "36 Times Obama Said You Could Keep Your Health Care Plan," *Washington Free Beacon* November 5, 2013, https://www.youtube.com/watch?v=qpa-5JdCnmo.

39 "Flashback: Obama's Health Care Cost Promises," BlackandRight, October 6, 2013, https://www.youtube.com/watch?v=LW9tPdpu2jY.

promised the American people that he would televise all his health care negotiations on C-SPAN, "so that people can see who is making arguments on behalf of their constituents, and who are making arguments on behalf of the drug companies or the insurance companies."[40] None of these so-called promises proved true.

If Sanders believes his claim that single payer will save American families money so fervently, then he should ask the Congressional Budget Office to analyze all the fiscal effects of his proposal. Because Sanders serves as ranking member of the Senate Budget Committee, CBO would almost certainly prioritize his request.

Sanders should also propose specific tax increases—not a menu of options, but drafted legislative language—necessary to fund the cost of the bill that CBO determines. Then, and only then, could scorekeepers at CBO and elsewhere analyze the veracity of Sanders's claims that most people will pay less.[41] That he's not willing to do this so far suggests he's only a politician trying to avoid telling the American people a politically inconvenient truth.

CAUTIONARY TALE FROM THE GREEN MOUNTAIN STATE

If Sanders wants evidence that single payer would destroy the economy through a series of devastating tax increases, he need look no further than his home state of Vermont. Late in 2014,

---

40   "President Obama Making C-SPAN Promise Eight Separate Times," Republican Study Committee January 6, 2010, https://www.youtube.com/watch?v=kPMf6kW_1Nw.

41   Chris Jacobs, "The CBO Report on Single Payer Isn't the One We Deserve to See," *The Federalist* May 3, 2018, https://thefederalist.com/2019/05/03/cbo-report-single-payer-isnt-one-deserve-see/.

Vermont's Democratic governor, Peter Shumlin, announced he could not move forward with his state's plan to create a single-payer system for the Green Mountain State.

As the *Washington Post* noted in a feature-length story about Vermont's failed experiment in socialized medicine, single-payer supporters fail to "acknowledg[e], let alone wrestl[e] with, the gritty complexities" needed to create such a system:

> Then as now, many of the advocates shared "a belief that borders on the theological" that such a system would save money, as one analyst put it—even though no one knew what it would cost when it passed in Vermont.
>
> That believe would prove naïve. The choices Shumlin favored would essentially have doubled Vermont's budget, raising state income taxes by up to 9.5 percent and placing an 11.5 percent payroll tax on employers—a burden Shumlin said would pose "a risk of an economic shock"—even though Vermonters would no longer pay for private health plans.[42]

In attempting to create a single-payer system, Vermont had many advantages that the United States as a whole does not. Vermont has a comparatively low uninsured rate, and a relatively homogenous and healthy population. Moreover, Vermont proposed a benefit plan covering "only" 94% of residents' health-care costs on average—as opposed to the House and Senate single-payer bills, which would cover virtually all of

---

42   Amy Goldstein, "Why Vermont's Single Payer Effort Failed, and What Democrats Can Learn from It," *Washington Post,* April 29, 2019, https://www.washingtonpost. com/national/health-science/why-vermonts-single-payer-effort-failed-and-what-democrats-can-learn-from-it/2019/04/29/c9789018-3ab8-11e9-a2cd-307b06d0257b_story.html?utm_term=.c8bce12aab07.

Americans' health spending without cost-sharing.[43]

Yet Shumlin admitted to the *Post* that "We were pretty shocked at the tax rates we were going to have to charge.[44] The tax increases discussed in Vermont—9.5% for the income tax, and 11.5% for payroll taxes—far exceed Sanders's proposed income and payroll tax increases of 4% and 7.5%, respectively.[45] Vermont's experience, like Thorpe's 2016 analysis of Sanders's plan (Thorpe also consulted on the Vermont plan), demonstrate that Sanders's current financing mechanisms likely come nowhere close to paying for a single-payer system's new spending.

Perhaps unsurprisingly, given the way that facts from his own state undercut his "theological" belief in socialized medicine, Sanders has said little about Vermont's failed single-payer experiment.[46] But Shumlin provided some wise, albeit unsolicited, advice to Sanders and his single-payer brethren: "If I were running for president of the United States, I would have a team working on a plan so I don't sell an idea to Americans that you can't achieve. That's the mistake I made."[47]

DESTRUCTIVE EFFECTS OF TAX INCREASES

Over and above whether people would pay more or less under single payer, the tax increases will have a major impact, as the deadweight losses from higher taxes will lead to lower overall

---

43   Ibid.

44   Ibid.

45   Sanders, "Financing Medicare for All."

46   Goldstein, "Why Vermont's Single Payer Effort Failed."

47   Ibid.

growth. A term frequently used by economists, deadweight losses refer to the inefficiencies that result from government taxation. For instance, a $100,000 per-passenger tax on airplane travel would yield next to no revenue, since most people would choose other forms of travel, but it would yield massive deadweight losses, because traveling by bus, rail, or boat would take much longer than travel by plane.[48] In other words, deadweight losses refer not just to a tax of money but also a tax on citizens' time and effort, which may be even more valuable.

The White House's Council of Economic Advisers (CEA) analyzed the ways single payer would profoundly affect economic growth. Specifically, the CEA model found that single payer would reduce national income and long-run GDP by 9%.[49] Regardless of what single-payer supporters claim their proposal would do to our nation's health-care system, it would make the American economy as a whole much smaller.

Total national income excluding taxes and health spending would fall by an even greater 19%, or about $17,000 per household.[50] Imagine losing that amount from your disposable income every year, after you pay the massive tax increases needed to fund this socialist scheme. As the CEA notes,

> [Single payer] is not just a swap of taxes for private health spending. Moving health spending onto the Federal budget reduces private sector economic activity so much that

---

48   Council of Economic Advisers, *Economic Report of the President*, March 2019, https://www.whitehouse.gov/wp-content/uploads/2019/03/ERP-2019.pdf, p. 227.

49   Ibid., pp. 424-25.

50   Ibid., Table 8-7, National Accounts With and Without "Medicare for All," 2022, p. 425.

households are spending 19 percent less on non-health items than they would be without [single payer].[51]

Single payer presents a triple whammy to the American people: It raises taxes on individuals and shrinks the non-health portion of the economy, thereby making health care more expensive by comparison.

Moreover, even this estimate of a 19% reduction in non-health spending does not consider all the deadweight effects of single payer on the American economy. For instance, the CEA model could not accurately capture the effects of the vast changes within the health-care sector, and the discouragement of innovation, that would accompany the transition to a single-payer system.[52] These changes will have undoubted economic impacts, and even more profound impacts on the quality of patient care, as later sections of this book will highlight.

SQUIRT GUN IN AN OCEAN

The single-payer bills do acknowledge the disruption this new system will inflict on the American economy. However, the proposed "solutions" to the problem seem vastly insufficient, demonstrating the foolishness of enacting the legislation to begin with.

In discussing the new national budget for health care, Section 601 of the Senate legislation includes the following language:

For up to 5 years following the date on which benefits first become available as described in section 106(a), up to 1

---

51   Ibid., p. 424.

52   Casey Mulligan, Council of Economic Advisers, personal communication, April 11, 2019.

percent of the budget may be allocated to programs providing assistance to workers who perform functions in the administration of the health insurance system and who may experience economic dislocation as a result of the implementation of this Act.[53]

The House bill includes similar language, although it states that the federal government "shall" allocate "at least 1 percent" of the health budget for a period of up to five years for job training.[54]

Regardless, assuming an expenditure of 1% of total health expenditures for five years, the amounts seem paltry compared to the scale of the need this program would create. In 2018, national health expenditures totaled $3.6 trillion.[55] Assuming modest inflation, spending 1% of national health spending on economic assistance would represent approximately $40-50 billion per year. Compare that to the impact of the legislation itself, based on some of the surveys and data cited:

- Up to 540,000 job losses within the insurance industry

- More than $150 billion in reduced revenue to hospitals, to say nothing of lower revenues to physician groups and other medical providers

- Between 900,000 and 1.5 million job reductions within the hospital sector alone, which again excludes physician groups and other medical providers

---

53   Section 601(a)(4) of S. 1129.

54   Section 601(a)(8)(A) of H.R. 1384.

55   CMS Office of the Actuary, "National Health Expenditure Projections."

The language in the House bill applies the transition fund only to those *directly* affected by single payer, but its harmful effects will trickle throughout the economy. The worker retraining funds will do nothing to compensate individuals for stock market losses due to the virtual elimination of for-profit medical providers, or the harmful effects of the tax increases needed to fund the new system. Nor would it address the knock-on effects of the law's dislocations—for instance, the café owner across from a hospital or insurance company who sees fewer lunch customers when the big employer next door has to lay off workers.

Just as the American people and economy are beginning to recover from the effects of the Great Recession, single payer could well lead to another period of prolonged stagnation and economic malaise. The extremely risky idea would inflict many varieties of pain upon Americans and, given the United States' global influence, upon the world.

Worst of all, single payer would likely inflict its harshest pain upon those least able to absorb it. Thorpe's 2016 analysis clearly demonstrates how, no matter how much Sanders or other supporters claim that "the rich" will pay for all or most of single payer's massive spending bill, the real burden will fall on poor and vulnerable Americans.

As it is, most lower-income Americans already qualify for "free" health care. Due to Obamacare's expansion of Medicaid to able-bodied adults, many can receive coverage with no premiums, deductibles, co-payments, or any other forms of cost-sharing. Therefore, any single-payer plan that raises their income or payroll taxes—even by as little as one dollar—will by definition make them worse off. Small wonder then that Thorpe concluded more than five in six (85%) Medicaid households would lose out under the Sanders plan.

Middle- and working-class Americans already face high (and rising) health costs, stagnant incomes, and the loss of jobs and economic vibrancy in many rural areas. But single payer would give them gut punch after gut punch: At least a 4% increase in their income taxes, at least a 7.5% increase in payroll taxes—which firms will of course pass on to their workers in the form of lower take-home pay—and millions of job losses to boot.

As with Obamacare, single-payer supporters hope they can highlight the very tangible "winners" from their proposal, while hiding any mention of the "losers." They would advertise newly insured individuals receiving care, while avoiding discussion of the jobs never created, the raises never granted, the rising tax bills that would increasingly eat away at families' hard-earned income and savings.

But to reiterate a point from the last chapter, single payer will cost taxpayers at least $32 trillion in the coming decade—and likely much more than that. No politician, however skilled in the art of rhetoric, could hide the ill effects of a program that massive. At some point, the reality of single payer would rapidly catch up to leftists' rhetoric. But better that American workers and businesses never become guinea pigs for socialists' failed theories in the first place.

REAPING THE KEYNESIAN WHIRLWIND

Over the past several years, liberals have cited Keynesian economic principles as one reason for recalcitrant states to embrace Obamacare's Medicaid expansion to the able-bodied. Bringing new federal dollars will grow jobs inside and outside the health sector, they claimed, benefiting a state's entire economy. The Obama administration even compiled a report claiming that expansion created 78,600 jobs in states that embraced it, and would create an additional 84,800 jobs if all states did so.[56]

Single payer would throw that "multiplier" calculus entirely on its head. Because liberals view single payer as a way to lower health spending, the new system would take money out of the economy, through the reductions in reimbursements to hospitals and other medical providers outlined above. According to Keynesian theory, those reductions would lead to negative effects—layoffs, or wage reductions, by hospitals and medical providers, leading to a reduction in spending among medical workers that would cascade throughout the economy.

Of course, "health care is not a jobs program." It exists to make people healthier.[57] If a hospital takes 20 people to do work easily performed by ten, the additional jobs "created" ultimately benefit neither the hospital nor the economy. The key question lies in whether spending on health care improves efficiency—by "achiev[ing] better health outcomes and improv[ing] overall economic productivity."[58]

On that front, single payer seems highly unlikely to deliver its promised benefits. Rather than allowing individuals to make their own choices about health-care consumption and quality, single payer will centralize those decisions in the hands of government

---

56 Council of Economic Advisers, "Missed Opportunities: The Consequences of State Decisions Not to Expand Medicaid," July 2014, https://obamawhitehouse.archives.gov/sites/default/files/docs/missed_opportunities_medicaid_0.pdf, p. 5.

57 Zeke Emanuel, "We Can Be Healthy and Rich," *New York Times,* February 2, 2013, https://opinionator.blogs.nytimes.com/2013/02/02/we-can-be-healthy-and-rich/.

58 Katherine Baicker and Amitabh Chandra, "The Health Care Jobs Fallacy," *New England Journal of Medicine,* June 28, 2012, https://wcfia.harvard.edu/files/wcfia/files/chandra_hc_jobs.pdf.

bureaucrats. Moreover, providing health care "free" to consumers will only encourage them to use more than they need while billing taxpayers, exacerbating the current problem in health care whereby individuals too easily spend other people's money.

From an economic perspective, single payer appears the worst of all possible worlds. Having increased demand, the system will constrain costs by arbitrarily limiting supply. Its lower reimbursements to doctors and hospitals, to say nothing of its elimination of private health insurance, will result in job losses in the short term. The dramatically higher taxes needed to fund single payer will drag on economic growth in the long term.

To top it off, implementing the new system will require a massive increase in federal authority and regulations, which will *also* hinder economic growth—and further entrench government bureaucrats in American health-care markets. As the next chapter shows, these bureaucrats have plenty other than your best interests in mind.

5

THE PROBLEMS WITH "DOCTOR SAM"

KEY POINTS

- Single-payer legislation proposes enormous grants of authority to the federal government, particularly to unelected bureaucrats.

- From giving bureaucrats the power to allocate trillions of dollars in spending, to forcing doctors to provide abortions, to creating massive databases, a single-payer system will centralize control of the entire health-care system in Washington.

- Because fraud and abuse plague existing government health programs, paying for all Americans through a single-payer system could turn a problem of improper or fraudulent payments costing taxpayers tens of billions annually into one costing *hundreds of billions* of dollars each year.

- The new authority granted to the federal government will also encourage crony capitalism—special-interest lobbyists pleading with officials to obtain additional government largesse.

- Single payer would only encourage the worst excesses of Washington, putting "the swamp" on steroids.

Under the rules of the House of Representatives, the majority and minority party leaders each have the privilege of assigning the first ten numbered bills of each Congress to their top legislative priorities.[1] For the 116th Congress, Speaker Nancy Pelosi (D-CA) designated as H.R. 1—her top priority—a bill called the "For the People Act." Passed by the House of Representatives on March 8, 2019, the bill claims to "reduce the influence of big money in politics, and strengthen ethics rules for public servants."[2]

Conservatives have numerous concerns about the legislation's provisions, for attempting to stifle the First Amendment rights of individuals and organizations in the name of "ethics reform." But over and above philosophical objections to the

---

1   Section 103(e) of H.Res. 6, Adopting the Rules of the House of Representatives for the 116th Congress, as passed by the House on January 3, 2019.

2   H.R. 1, as passed by the House of Representatives on March 8, 2019; House Roll Call Vote 118 of 2019, http://clerk.house.gov/evs/2019/roll118.xml.

measure, supporters of the ethics legislation fail to comprehend that single-payer health care would undermine most, if not all, of the supposed "reforms" in H.R. 1.

Single payer would invest the federal government with enormous power, even compared to its current sizable influence. The legislation would incorporate trillions of dollars of new spending into the federal sphere, and give unelected bureaucrats the power to write new rules affecting every corner of the health-care market. With health care currently comprising 17.9% of the economy, and rising, single payer would give federal officials command and control over a vast swath of our society.[3]

Almost by definition, this new federal authority presents an invitation to corruption of all kinds. Fraudsters would seek to make a quick buck by submitting claims for improperly provided goods and services, as they do regularly in the current Medicare and Medicaid programs.

Under single payer, every doctor, hospital, drug manufacturer, and other medical provider would have an even greater incentive to hire lobbyists to increase their reimbursements from the government, which would represent most providers' largest source of income, if not their *only* source of income. Rather than draining "the swamp" in Washington, single payer would only make the federal cesspool worse.

Democrats in Congress need not look far to find the corrupting effects of such government power on the political process. The sordid tale of their colleague Sen. Robert Menendez

---

3   Centers for Medicare and Medicaid Services Office of the Actuary, "National Health Expenditure Projections 2018-2027: Forecast Summary," February 20, 2019, https://www.cms.gov/Research-Statistics-Data-and-Systems/Statistics-Trends-and-Reports/NationalHealthExpendData/Downloads/ForecastSummary.pdf.

(D-NJ), tried for corruption to his links with physician and convicted fraudster Salomon Melgen, provides a clear example of how federal involvement in health care foments improper influence-peddling. These trends would only accelerate under a single-payer system, no matter how many "ethics reform" bills Congress may pass.

THE MOST EGREGIOUS POWER GRABS

Single payer's entire premise focuses on consolidating power within government. The House and Senate bills contain numerous specific provisions giving the federal government—specifically bureaucrats working on the federal government's behalf—tremendous authority. Examining some of its most egregious provisions demonstrates how single payer will take authority from patients—and doctors and hospitals—and hand it to unelected officials in Washington.

Requiring Doctors to Provide Abortions: Section 104 of the House and Senate single-payer bills includes provisions prohibiting discrimination—a laudable goal, in theory. However, the text of the bill could have far more troubling implications for medical providers:

> No person shall, on the basis of race, color, national origin, age, disability, marital status, citizenship status, or…sex, including…pregnancy and related conditions (including termination of pregnancy), be excluded from participation in or be denied the benefits of the program…or be subject to any reduction of benefits or other discrimination by any participating provider.[4]

---

4   Section 104(a) of H.R. 1384 and S. 1129, the Medicare for All Act of 2019.

This language would effectively define doctors who refuse to perform abortions as engaging in discrimination, for "den[ying] the benefits of the program" on the basis of "pregnancy and related conditions (including termination of pregnancy)." Under the bill, the more than 600 Catholic hospitals nationwide—who treat more than one in seven American patients—could face severe penalties, or even termination from the program, for refusing to provide taxpayer-funded abortion-on-demand.[5]

Obamacare contains similar non-discrimination provisions that have resulted in legal controversy.[6] After the Obama administration interpreted the provisions to include gender identity, religiously affiliated employers sued. A federal district court judge struck down the provision, although appeals, and an attempt by the Trump administration to rewrite the relevant regulations, remain ongoing.[7]

Despite its controversial non-discrimination language, Obamacare contained a provision stating that nothing in the law would "be construed to have any effect" on existing federal law securing conscience protections.[8] That federal law, in the form of a prohibition attached to Congress's annual spending

---

5   Catholic Health Association, "U.S. Catholic Health Care 2019," https://www. chausa.org/docs/default-source/default-document-library/cha_2019_miniprofile. pdf?sfvrsn=0.

6   Section 1557 of the Patient Protection and Affordable Care Act, P.L. 111-148, codified at 42 U.S.C. 18116.

7   Anna Gorman, "Obamacare Now Pays for Gender Reassignment," *Daily Beast,* August 25, 2014, https://www.thedailybeast.com/obamacare-now-pays-for-gender-reassignment; Katie Keith, "ACA Litigation Round-Up: Take Care, Contraceptive Mandate, Section 1557, and HIT," *Health Affairs* blog, March 22, 2019, https://www. healthaffairs.org/do/10.1377/hblog20190322.945198/full/.

8   Section 1303(c)(2) of PPACA, codified at 42 U.S.C. 18023(c)(2).

bills, prohibits any government entity from "subject[ing] any institutional or individual health care entity to discrimination on the basis that the health care entity does not provide, pay for, provide coverage of, or refer for abortions."[9]

However, the single-payer bills provide an entirely separate and new source of funds for the new government-run health system. As a result, most existing conscience protections for medical providers would not apply.[10] Under single payer, doctors and hospitals would be forced to provide abortions and other services that violate their deeply held religious beliefs.

Ethics Requirements Run Amok: Section 301 of the House bill states that board members, executives, and administrators of providers like hospitals or nursing homes may not "receive compensation from, own stock or [have] other financial investments in, or serve as a board member of any entity that contracts with or provides items and services, including pharmaceutical products

---

9   See for instance Section 507(d)(1) of Division B of the Department of Defense and Labor, Health and Human Services, and Education Appropriations Act, 2019 and Continuing Appropriations Act, 2019, P.L. 115-245.

10   Beyond the annual appropriations rider, known as the Weldon Amendment, a separate conscience provision exists in permanent federal law. This provision, known as the Church Amendment, is codified at 42 U.S.C. 300a-7. The Church Amendment prohibits grant recipients under three statutes—the Public Health Service Act, the Community Mental Health Centers Act, and the Developmental Disabilities Services and Facilities Construction Act—from taking actions against employees who refuse to perform abortion or sterilization procedures. A further provision of the Church Amendment applies similar restrictions to any biomedical or behavioral research grant administered by HHS. While these conscience provisions may appear robust at first glance, they apply to a comparatively small amount of federal funding, making their ultimate applicability limited. Moreover, if the grants funded under these programs get subsumed into the single-payer system, as the program's adherents undoubtedly hope, even these limited conscience protections will no longer apply.

and medical devices or equipment, to such provider."[11] While this provision intends to combat conflicts of interest, its broad language would likely encompass otherwise-innocuous behavior.

For instance, a strict reading of this provision in the House bill would prohibit any hospital executive or board member from holding stock in pharmaceutical or other health-care companies. In some cases, individuals might not even know that their mutual funds hold stock in health-care-related entities, but could get ensnared by this provision regardless.

Massive Government Database: Section 401 of the House and Senate bills requires the secretary of Health and Human Services to create "an adequate national database" containing information related to:

1. "Health services practitioners,"

2. "Approved providers,"

3. "The costs of facilities and practitioners providing items and services,"

4. "The quality of such…services,"

5. "The outcomes of such…services, and"

6. "The equity of health among population groups."[12]

The House bill contains more specific language on what information participating providers will have to give the federal government to compile this database, in addition to the data they are already providing under existing federal requirements:

---

11   Section 301(b)(1)(I) of H.R. 1384. See also Section 301(b)(2)(C).

12   Section 401(b)(1)(A) of H.R. 1384 and S. 1129.

1. "Annual financial data that includes information on employees (including the number of employees, hours worked, and wage information) by job title and by each patient care unit or department within each facility (including outpatient units or departments);"

2. "The number of registered nurses per staffed bed by each such unit or department";

3. "Information on the dollar value and annual spending (including purchases, upgrades, and maintenance) for health information technology; and"

4. "Risk-adjusted and raw patient outcome data (including data on medical, surgical, obstetric, and other procedures)."[13]

The breathtaking scope contemplated for this database poses several questions, including whether it would even work. Recall that not too many years ago, the federal government spent more than $2 billion building a website to facilitate enrollment in Obamacare, and that website famously crashed and burned on its launch.[14] Given that catastrophic failure, who should believe this even-more-ambitious venture in government technology would lead to a different outcome?

The privacy of this "adequate national database" raises another obvious issue. The House and Senate bills both include language about releasing outcome measures and other information from

---

13   Section 401(b)(1)(B)(ii) of H.R. 1384.

14   Alex Wayne, "Obamacare Website Costs Exceed $2 Billion, Study Finds," *Bloomberg*, September 24, 2014, https://www.bloomberg.com/news/articles/2014-09-24/obamacare-website-costs-exceed-2-billion-study-finds.

the database "without compromising patient privacy."[15]

But even though the House bill contains detailed requirements for reporting on employees—including job titles, wages,
and hours worked—it includes not a word about *employees'* privacy. The nonchalant way the legislation disregards any possible
privacy concerns about millions of health-care employees suggests the federal government would disregard patients' privacy
in a similar manner, notwithstanding the nods to patient privacy
included in the bill. The federal government already disregards
privacy concerns in many of the databases it oversees.[16]

Most importantly, however, this database implies that the
federal government can, and should, supervise and oversee
thousands of hospitals, and hundreds of thousands of other
medical providers, nationwide. Over and above whether such
micro-management would work in practice, few doctors, let
alone patients, would welcome the idea that federal bureaucrats—the proverbial "Doctor Sam"—are constantly looking
over their shoulders, in ways that intrude upon the doctor-
patient relationship.

The ongoing debacle over health information technology
speaks to the ultimately harmful, however well-intentioned,
efforts of government bureaucrats to interfere in the practice

---

15   Section 401(b)(1)(C) of H.R. 1384.

16   Jane Robbins, Joy Pullmann, and Emmett McGroarty, "Cogs in the Machine: Big
     Data, Common Core, and National Testing," Pioneer Institute White Paper No. 114,
     May 2014, http://pioneerinstitute.org/wp-content/uploads/dlm_uploads/Cogs-in-
     the-Machine_new.pdf.

of medicine.[17] As a 2019 *Fortune* magazine exposé noted, doctors now spend more time per day interacting with screens, in the form of electronic health records, than they do with actual patients.[18] Tens of billions of dollars of government spending, as part of the 2009 economic "stimulus," forced hospitals to buy health IT systems that weren't ready for prime time, just to meet government requirements.

While proponents of the government spending spree claimed that electronic health records would save money and time, they have done the opposite. One study concluded that an emergency room doctor makes an average of 4,000 mouse clicks in the course of a single shift, a sum that virtually guarantees human errors by turning highly trained physicians into button-pushing automatons.[19]

Electronic health records have caused at least 101 deaths from various forms of "alert fatigue," and likely many more not officially documented.[20] This failed experiment speaks volumes about projects like the "adequate national database" proposed in single-payer legislation, and its questionable chance of success. Moreover, as the electronic health records debacle demonstrates, sometimes even when projects "succeed"—most doctors and hospitals now do use electronic health records, because the

---

17 Chris Jacobs, "How Electronic Health Records Became an Absolute Fiasco," *The Federalist,* April 30, 2019, https://thefederalist.com/2019/04/30/electronic-health-records-became-absolute-fiasco/.

18 Erika Fry and Fred Schulte, "Death by a Thousand Clicks: Where Electronic Health Records Went Wrong," *Fortune,* March 18, 2019, http://fortune.com/longform/medical-records/.

19 Ibid.

20 Ibid.

federal government forces them to—unintended consequences can nevertheless create a massive failure.

Allocating Trillions of Dollars: Section 601 of the House bill directs the secretary of Health and Human Services to allocate the national health budget thusly:

> (3) ALLOCATION AMONG COMPONENTS.—The Secretary shall allocate the funds received for purposes of carrying out this Act among the components described in paragraph (2) in a manner that ensures—
>
> (A) that the operating budget allows for every participating provider in the Medicare for All Program to meet the needs of their respective patient populations;
>
> (B) that the special projects budget is sufficient to meet the health care needs within areas described in paragraph (2)(C) through the construction, renovation, and staffing of health care facilities in a reasonable timeframe;
>
> (C) a fair allocation for quality assessment activities; and
>
> (D) that the health professional education expenditure component is sufficient to provide for the amount of health professional education expenditures sufficient to meet the need for covered health care services.[21]

---

21   Section 601(a)(3) of H.R. 1384.

In 2018, Americans spent more than $3.6 trillion—that's $3,600,000,000,000—on health care.[22] A single-payer system would bring virtually all that spending onto the federal government's already grossly unbalanced books. Only the 128 words outlined above would provide guidance to HHS on where, and how, to spend that money. And the House bill seems practically verbose in comparison to the Senate legislation, which includes a mere 58 words directing HHS on how to spend trillions of dollars.[23]

Other provisions within the legislation give HHS similarly broad authority to determine spending allocations. The House bill directs the secretary to "provide each regional office with an allotment the Secretary determines appropriate" to carry out the program—giving one individual the unilateral, and virtually limitless, authority to set spending levels for the various regional health systems.[24] Likewise, when determining payment amounts for hospitals, the House bill also gives the secretary the authority to consider "any other factor determined appropriate."[25]

These virtually unchecked grants of authority to a single individual, or a group of unelected bureaucrats, give HHS carte blanche to remake the health system however its unelected leadership likes. Particularly given the ways liberals have criticized

---

22 Centers for Medicare and Medicaid Services Office of the Actuary, "National Health Expenditure Projections 2018-2027: ," https://www.cms.gov/Research-Statistics-Data-and-Systems/Statistics-Trends-and-Reports/NationalHealthExpendData/Downloads/Proj2018Tables.zip, Table 2, National Health Expenditure Amounts and Annual Percent Change by Type of Expenditure: Calendar Years 2011-2027.

23 Section 601(a)(3) of S. 1129.

24 Section 601(a)(5) of H.R. 1384.

25 Section 611(b)(2)(H) of H.R. 1384.

President Trump for his implementation of Obamacare, one would question why this legislation provides even more authority to the executive branch, and therefore more opportunities for such supposed "sabotage."[26]

Allowing the Executive to Legislate: Section 701 of the House legislation contains provisions regarding the new single-payer system's funding. After establishing the level of appropriations for the program's first year, the bill includes the following about future years' spending levels:

> (B) SUBSEQUENT YEARS.—Notwithstanding any other provision of law, there is appropriated to the trust fund for the fiscal year containing January 1 of the second year following the date of the enactment of this Act, and for each fiscal year thereafter, an amount equal to the amount appropriated to the Trust Fund for the previous year, adjusted for reductions in costs resulting from the implementation of this Act, changes in the consumer price index for all urban consumers for the fiscal year involved, and *other factors determined appropriate by the Secretary*. [Emphasis added.][27]

The Constitution specifically states that "No money shall be drawn from the Treasury, but in consequence of appropriations made by law."[28] In fact, House Democrats objected to President Trump's border emergency declaration for precisely this reason.

---

26 Andy Slavitt, "Going on Offense to Save Obamacare from Trump Sabotage: It's Illegal and Unconstitutional," *USA Today*, August 2, 2018, https://www.usatoday.com/story/opinion/2018/08/02/lawsuit-trump-obamacare-sabotage-illegal-and-unconstitutional-column/873306002/.

27 Section 701(b)(2)(B) of H.R. 1384.

28 Article I, Section 9, Clause 7 of the United States Constitution.

House Speaker Nancy Pelosi wrote that the border declaration "undermines the separation of powers and Congress's power of the purse, a power exclusively reserved by the text of the Constitution to the first branch of government, the legislative branch, a branch co-equal to the executive."[29]

But Section 701 of the House's single-payer bill would effectively grant the secretary of HHS the authority—authority Pelosi rightly notes belongs in the hands of Congress—to appropriate funds. By creating whatever "adjustments" he or she finds "appropriate," the secretary can thereby set appropriations levels—a "power of the purse" that the Constitution reserves to Congress. Whereas President Trump's emergency declaration resulted in a transfer of approximately $6.6 billion toward border security, the grant of spending authority the bill would give to the secretary of Health and Human Services will affect trillions of dollars in federal spending.[30]

Stifling First Amendment Rights: Section 614 of the House bill includes language prohibiting payments to providers from taking into account, or being used for, "any agreement or arrangement described in Section 203(a)(4) of the Labor-Management Reporting and Disclosure Act of 1959."[31] That section of law describes "any agreement or arrangement with

---

29   Rep. Nancy Pelosi, "Dear Colleague: All Members Encouraged to Co-sponsor Congressman Castro's Privileged Resolution to Terminate President Trump's Emergency Declaration," February 21, 2019, https://www.speaker.gov/newsroom/22119/.

30   The White House, "President Donald J. Trump's Border Security Victory," February 15, 2019, https://www.whitehouse.gov/briefings-statements/president-donald-j-trumps-border-security-victory/.

31   Section 614(b)(4) of H.R. 1384.

a labor relations consultant" who "undertakes such activities where an object thereof, directly or indirectly, is to persuade employees to exercise or not to exercise…the right to organize and bargain collectively."[32] By prohibiting doctors and hospitals from using funds to educate employees about the pros and cons of unionization, the House bill attempts to stifle medical providers' First Amendment rights to free speech.

Seizing Intellectual Property: Section 616 of the House bill states that the secretary of Health and Human Services shall "negotiate" pharmaceutical prices with drug manufacturers. However, if "the Secretary is unable to successfully negotiate an appropriate price" with a manufacturer—the term "appropriate" defined by the secretary, of course—he or she must override any government patents or exclusivities the manufacturer holds, and grant a license to other companies to produce the drug for the government health program.[33] The bill requires those other companies to provide "reasonable" compensation to the original manufacturer holding the patents, but leaves the secretary to define that "reasonable compensation."[34]

One study found that drug manufacturers spend an average of nearly $1.4 billion out of pocket to bring a new pharmaceutical to market.[35] After factoring in opportunity costs, meaning

---

32 Section 203(a)(4) of the Labor and Management Reporting and Disclosure Act, codified at 29 U.S.C. 433(a)(4).

33 Section 616(3)(A) of H.R. 1384.

34 Ibid.

35 Joseph DiMasi, Henry Grabowski, and Ronald Hansen, "Innovation in the Pharmaceutical Industry: New Estimates of R&D Costs," *Journal of Health Economics,* May 2016, https://www.sciencedirect.com/science/article/abs/pii/S0167629616000291?via%3Dihub.

the money that companies might have earned had they invested that $1.4 billion elsewhere, the total cost of developing a new drug approaches $2.6 billion.[36] If companies believe they will not have an opportunity to recover those costs, or if that opportunity will depend upon the whims of what an HHS secretary considers "reasonable compensation," they will never invest time and resources to develop new, and potentially lifesaving, drugs in the first place.

This proposal will leave behind the millions of Americans—for instance, cancer patients fighting that deadly disease—whose quality of life and sometimes whole lives depend on medical innovation. While this provision in the House bill theoretically gives government bureaucrats tremendous power over drug manufacturers, in practice it may simply destroy the sector instead.

SINGLE PAYER A "FRAUDSTER'S PARADISE"

With apologies to Coolio, a new single-payer system could represent a dream come true for individuals wishing to pursue a career in fraud. Existing government health programs already face myriad problems with improper payments; expanding government-run health care to all Americans would only turbocharge the incentives for criminals to bilk taxpayers out of even more dollars.

In 2009, the television news magazine *60 Minutes* looked into what has become a $60 billion-per-year industry: Medicare fraud.[37] The report revealed shocking details about how fraud went from a cottage industry to big business for criminals:

---

36   Ibid.

37   Steve Kroft, "Medicare Fraud: A $60 Billion Crime," *60 Minutes,* October 23, 2009, https://www.cbsnews.com/news/medicare-fraud-a-60-billion-crime-23-10-2009/.

- A former federal judge received Medicare statements charging him for two artificial limbs, even though the judge has full use of his arms and legs. Criminals had submitted fraudulent bills in his name.

- One former fraudster admitted that "every day" he felt like he "just won the lottery," making tens of thousands of dollars stealing from Medicare. He estimated that in Miami alone, thousands of equipment suppliers were bilking Medicare.

- Eric Holder, when attorney general, admitted that "it's been pretty easy" to steal from Medicare: Criminals had "found a way to get pretty substantial amounts of money with not a huge amount of effort." Criminals had also found Medicare fraud more lucrative—and less risky— than dealing drugs: "The chances of being incarcerated were lower, the amount of time you would spend in jail was smaller."

- Medicare's director of program integrity conceded that "we have a program that pays out over a billion claims a year, over $430 billion, and our oversight budget has been extremely limited."[38]

Lest anyone think much has changed within the Medicare program in the decade since that report, the spring of 2019 saw not one but two separate billion-dollar fraud schemes exposed. In one, federal authorities obtained the conviction of Philip Esformes for orchestrating a $1.3 billion fraud scheme in which

---

38   Ibid.

he referred patients to nursing facilities so the facilities could bill Medicare and Medicaid for treatments the patients didn't need or never received.[39] In the second, federal authorities arrested and charged more than two dozen individuals with billing Medicare for $1.2 billion in orthopedic braces that recipients didn't need—just two days after Esformes's conviction.[40]

Since *60 Minutes* reported on Medicare fraud ten years ago, the program remains on the Government Accountability Office (GAO) "high-risk" list of programs susceptible to waste, fraud, and abuse, and has been since the list's creation in 1990.

Over the past two years, improper payments in Medicare—representing payments made incorrectly, or fraudulent payments that should not have been made at all—declined by 1 percentage point across the program.[41] However, Medicare has yet to implement 80 separate recommendations government auditors suggested to reduce fraud, and improper payments still totaled $48.5 billion during fiscal year 2018.[42]

While Medicare contains the largest share of federal government improper payments, another federal health program—Medicaid—ranks in second place. In fiscal year 2018, the two

---

39 Charisse Jones, "South Florida Businessman Convicted in $1.3 Billion Medicare and Medicaid Scheme," *USA Today,* April 7, 2019, https://www.usatoday.com/story/money/2019/04/07/businessman-found-guilty-1-3-billion-medicare-and-medicaid-scheme/3393975002/.

40 Ricardo Alonso-Zaldivar, "Feds Charge Two Dozen in Billion Dollar Medicare Brace Scam," *U.S. News & World Report,* April 9, 2019, https://www.usnews.com/news/business/articles/2019-04-09/feds-say-12b-medicare-back-brace-scam-busted.

41 Government Accountability Office, "High-Risk Series: Substantial Efforts Needed to Achieve Greater Progress on High-Risk Areas," Report GAO-19-157SP, March 6, 2019, https://www.gao.gov/assets/700/697245.pdf, p. 33.

42 Ibid., pp. 33-34.

programs combined for more than half (56.3%) of all improper payments within the federal government.[43] Like Medicare, Medicaid remains on GAO's "high-risk" list, where it has remained since 2003.

In fiscal year 2018, improper payments totaled $36.2 billion—nearly one in ten (9.8%) federal dollars spent on the program.[44] Yet despite the high rate of fraudulent and improper payments, more than one-quarter of recommendations by government auditors to improve Medicaid integrity remain unfulfilled.[45] Why would we expand programs that are this susceptible to fraud and impervious to improvement?

Single-payer advocates believe that creating a government-run health system would lead to administrative cost savings, both because of greater efficiency—doctors could use a single billing system and so forth—and elimination of the profit motive. But consider that the nation's largest health insurers made $21.7 billion in net profits in 2018, according to *Fortune* magazine.[46]

By comparison, Medicare and Medicaid—where government programs pay claims quickly, then try to chase fraudsters after the fact—incurred a total of $84.7 billion in improper or fraudulent payments, $48.5 billion from Medicare and $36.2

---

43   Ibid., Figure 7, Improper Payment Estimates Were Concentrated in These Areas in Fiscal Year 2018, p. 64.

44   Ibid., p. 250.

45   Ibid., p. 250.

46   Total includes profits by UnitedHealthGroup ($10.558 billion), Anthem ($3.843 billion), Aetna ($1.904 billion), Humana ($2.448 billion), Centene ($828 million), Cigna ($2.237 billion), Molina Health Care (loss of $512 million), and WellCare Health Plans ($374 million). See "Fortune 500," *Fortune*, http://fortune.com/fortune500/.

billion from Medicaid. Viewed from this prism, the $21.7 billion in insurer profits seems like a comparative bargain, particularly if private insurers do a better job not just of detecting fraud, but preventing it before crooks can get their hands on reimbursement checks.

Creating a single-payer system would invite a further explosion of health care fraud. In fiscal year 2018, the traditional Medicare fee-for-service program had an improper payment rate of 8.12%, while the Medicaid program had an improper payment rate of 9.8%.[47]

In 2018, Americans spent nearly $3.65 trillion on health care.[48] If a single-payer system in control of all that health spending maintains an improper payment rate equal to the current fee-for-service Medicare program, that would imply approximately $296.1 billion in spending on fraudulent or improper payments every year ($3.65 trillion multiplied by 8.12%). Conversely, if the single-payer system leads to an improper payment rate equal to the current Medicaid program, that would imply approximately $357.3 billion in spending on fraudulent or improper payments every year ($3.65 trillion multiplied by 9.8%).

---

47   GAO, "High-Risk Series," pp. 243 and 250. In fiscal year 2018, the Medicare Advantage and Medicare Part D programs had improper payment rates of 8.1% and 1.66%, respectively. However, because private insurers deliver these programs to seniors, and because the single-payer bills would make private health insurance "unlawful," the improper payment rate for traditional, fee-for-service Medicare provides the best point of comparison.

48   CMS Office of the Actuary, "National Health Expenditure Projections," Table 2.

By comparison, in 2018 the gross domestic product of Denmark totaled approximately $350.9 billion, while the GDP of Finland totaled $275.3 billion.[49] That improper health-care payments alone under an American single-payer system could exceed the *entire economies* of major developed countries, both of whom happen to have their own single-payer systems, speaks to the rampant problems in our existing government-run health programs. Yet neither the House nor Senate single-payer bill includes any major new provisions or ideas to crack down on health-care fraud, virtually ensuring that it will continue, and likely increase, under a new, larger, system.

"THE SWAMP" ON STEROIDS

Over and above explicit fraud, single payer would also lead to an increase in crony capitalism and special-interest lobbying. Under single payer, medical providers would have even more reason to hire lobbyists and plead for special treatment from the government-run system—likely most doctors' and hospitals' only source of revenue.

Consider the case of Sen. Bob Menendez. In 2015, federal prosecutors indicted the senator for a series of charges relating to bribery, fraud, and making false statements. In laying out their case against Menendez, prosecutors argued that he had become the "personal senator" to Salomon Melgen, a friend and ophthalmologist.[50] Menendez helped Melgen in his dealings

---

49   International Monetary Fund, "World Economic Outlook Database," April 2019, https://www.imf.org/external/pubs/ft/weo/2019/01/weodata/index.aspx.

50   Nick Corasaniti, "Opening Arguments in Menendez Trial Focus on the Meaning of Friendship," *New York Times*, September 6, 2017, https://www.nytimes.com/2017/09/06/nyregion/senator-robert-menendez-trial-melgen.html.

with the federal government while receiving nearly $1 million in gifts and favors, none of which he revealed on his required financial disclosure forms:

- "Flights on Melgen's private jet, a first-class commercial flight and a flight on a chartered jet;"

- "Numerous vacations at Melgen's Caribbean villa in the Dominican Republic and at a hotel room in Paris; and"

- "$40,000 in contributions to [Menendez's] legal defense fund and over $750,000 in campaign contributions."[51]

Some of the trial centered on Menendez's efforts to procure a port security contract for Melgen's company and obtain visas for his girlfriends. But health care, specifically Medicare, consumed a large portion of the case. Medicare officials sought nearly $9 million in repayments from Melgen, charging that he had overbilled the government program for the macular degeneration drug Lucentis.[52]

Menendez's corruption trial revealed the ways the senator personally intervened with Medicare officials, including the secretary of Health and Human Services, to help his friend Melgen. One Medicare official, recounting a 2009 phone call with the senator, said Menendez "was so angry that [he] wasn't

---

51   United States Department of Justice, "Senator Robert Menendez and Salomon Melgen Indicted for Conspiracy, Bribery, and Honest Services Fraud," April 1, 2015, https://www.justice.gov/opa/pr/senator-robert-menendez-and-salomon-melgen-indicted-conspiracy-bribery-and-honest-services.

52   Matt Friedman, "Testimony: 'Angry' Menendez Hung Up on Bureaucrat Who Wouldn't Help Melgen," *Politico*, October 2, 2017, https://www.politico.com/states/new-jersey/story/2017/10/02/angry-menendez-hung-up-on-bureaucrat-who-wouldnt-help-co-defendant-testimony-114817.

giving him the answers he wanted on his friend's Medicare billing dispute that he hung up on him."[53]

The official testified: "I was very curious why the senator was focused on this case and asked the staff several times. The senator is from New Jersey. The physician is based in Florida. I pressed our staff several times on the connection between the senator and Dr. Melgen."[54]

Three years later, Menendez was still trying to help his friend and contributor Melgen—this time with Obama's secretary of Health and Human Services, Kathleen Sebelius. Sebelius testified at Menendez's trial that she had attended a meeting in 2012 where Menendez again pressed the same issue he had three years earlier—the Medicare billing dispute about Melgen's use of the drug Lucentis. Sebelius testified about the unusual nature of the meeting—it came at the behest of Senate Majority Leader Harry Reid (D-NV), and it involved billing disputes normally handled by lower-ranking staff members.[55]

In the end, the jury deadlocked on whether to convict Menendez of the charges against him. Prosecutors ended up dropping the case entirely, in part due to the difficulty of proving an explicit quid pro quo in bribery and corruption cases.[56] But that does not mean the characters involved in the

---

53   Ibid.

54   Ibid.

55   Matt Friedman, "Sebelius Believed Menendez Wanted Her to 'Take Some Action,'" *Politico*, October 3, 2017, https://www.politico.com/states/new-jersey/story/2017/10/03/sebelius-menendez-wanted-me-to-do-something-114850.

56   Matt Friedman and Ryan Hutchins, "Justice Department Drops Corruption Case against Menendez," *Politico*, January 31, 2018, https://www.politico.com/story/2018/01/31/dismissal-of-menendez-case-380230.

case acted appropriately—to the contrary, in fact. The Senate Ethics Committee "severely admonished" Menendez for his behavior, and a federal jury convicted Melgen of defrauding the Medicare program out of $90 million.[57]

That a U.S. senator accepted nearly $1 million in gifts from a physician convicted of 67 separate counts of defrauding Medicare says much about the incestuous relationship between money and corruption already present in official Washington. Increasing Washington's authority, by making the federal government virtually omnipotent over health care, would only increase this kind of potential for corruption, and make that corruption worse.

AN INVITATION TO CORRUPTION

More than two centuries ago, James Madison famously wrote in *The Federalist Papers* that "If men were angels, no government would be necessary."[58] He continued, articulating one of the many problems with a single-payer system:

> In framing a government which is to be administered by men over men, the great difficulty lies in this: You must first enable the government to control the governed; and in the next place oblige it to control itself.[59]

---

57   United States Senate Select Committee on Ethics, "Public Letter of Admonition," April 26, 2018, https://www.ethics.senate.gov/public/index.cfm/files/serve?File_ id=49C12C75-7A26-4FE6-B070-19FCEF4D7532; United States Department of Justice, "South Florida Doctor Convicted of Sixty-Seven Criminal Counts Related to Medicare Fraud Scheme," April 28, 2017, https://www.justice.gov/usao-sdfl/pr/ south-florida-doctor-convicted-sixty-seven-criminal-counts-related-medicare-fraud.

58   *Federalist*, No. 51.

59   Ibid.

In advocating for a system of checks and balances, Madison hoped that, as he put it, personal ambition would counteract personal ambition, resulting in something approaching equilibrium among the various branches of government. Distributing power among many interests and people would help keep them all naturally accountable.

But single-payer legislation gives virtually unchecked power to one branch of government—and unelected bureaucrats at that. This large grant of power will lead to bureaucrats intervening in the doctor-patient relationship, to be sure. But it will also encourage two distinct types of corruption: Fraudulent schemes, whereby criminals steal directly from the government, and influence peddling, where special interests use lobbying and political "grease" to increase their share of taxpayer largesse.

The left believes that, after having made government omnipotent over vast stretches of society, it can impose enough constraints on the people administering that government to ensure its honest functioning. But Madison's theory, to say nothing of the practical history of rampant Medicare and Medicaid fraud, demonstrates otherwise.

Human experience shows that only making centralized government smaller and less powerful can control the inherent threat of corruption. Conversely, a single-payer health system would only make that threat worse.

6

SINGLE PAYER'S ROAD TO HEALTH-CARE RATIONING

KEY POINTS

- Making health care a "human right" means government has the "right" to tell you what health care you will and will *not* receive.

- Because single payer will increase people's use of health care, government will have to contain costs by limiting the supply of care provided.

- Much lower pay will cause doctors to leave the profession, worsening the doctor shortages expected as Baby Boom physicians retire.

- The House's single-payer bill would provide hospitals a set budget every quarter, potentially forcing them to deny care to stay within their allocated budgets.

- Many single-payer supporters, including President Obama, have spoken favorably about controlling access to costly treatments to save money.

- In addition to limiting access to costly care, single payer will also allow for taxpayer funding of abortion at any time during a pregnancy and for any reason, undermining a culture of life nationwide.

Liberals don't talk about it much, but making health care a "human right" comes with a big downside.

To make health care a human right, as Sen. Bernie Sanders frequently claims a single-payer system will do, the federal government will have to *define* that right. And by defining what health care individuals will receive, a single-payer system—especially one that prohibits private insurance outside the government system, as the House and Senate bills do—will also define what care individuals will *not* receive.

As we have seen, by making health care a "human right," a single-payer system will lead to large increases in people using health care. The combination of 1) more insured patients, 2) more covered services, and 3) the abolition of cost-sharing for all health care services will cause demand to soar.

How, then, can government accommodate all this new demand? In a word, it won't. Instead, government bureaucrats will attempt to contain health care costs by restricting the supply of care provided.

That rationing will take on several forms. In some cases,

physicians will quit, or never enter medical school in the first place, reducing the available supply of care. In other cases, the global budget model introduced in the House's single-payer bill will encourage hospitals to stint on care to meet their government-set spending targets. In other cases, the government could outright deny treatments federal bureaucrats deem too expensive.

In all cases, however, the limits on access to care will have very real consequences for patients, particularly elderly seniors with multiple chronic conditions. When coupled with the bill's provisions on abortion, which allow for taxpayer-funded abortion-on-demand, single payer will end up abandoning some of our society's most vulnerable individuals.

Even single-payer supporters admit their legislation will ration health care.[1] When the Mercatus Center released its study questioning the costs of a single-payer system, a writer for the socialist magazine *Jacobin* responded:

> [The study] assumes utilization of health services will increase by 11 percent, but aggregate health service utilization is ultimately dependent on the capacity to provide services, meaning utilization could hit a hard limit below the level [the study] projects.[2]

---

1   Chris Jacobs, "Bernie Sanders Supporters Admit His Socialized Medicine Plan Will Ration Care," *The Federalist* August 2, 2018, http://thefederalist.com/2018/08/02/bernie-sanders-supporters-admit-socialized-medicine-plan-will-ration-care/.

2   Matt Bruenig, "Even Libertarians Admit Medicare for All Would Save Trillions," *Jacobin,* July 30, 2018, https://www.jacobinmag.com/2018/07/medicare-for-all-mercatus-center-report.

This socialist commentator knows of which he speaks. Both the liberal Urban Institute and Rand Corporation assume that demand for health care will increase under a single-payer system, raising health-care spending—but that constraints on supply will prevent many people from accessing all the additional care they seek.[3]

It seems little surprise, then, that Sanders's rhetoric about single payer notwithstanding, neither the House nor the Senate single-payer bills actually make health care a right.[4] Instead of guaranteeing the right to receive health care, they only guarantee the right to have that care paid for if Americans can find someone to provide it in the first place—a major catch Sanders never mentions.[5]

Sanders must rely on this legal sleight-of-hand to sell his plan. He, like other single-payer supporters, recognizes that the plan will limit the health care provided to Americans, because supply in the system won't keep up with demand. Here's how they will do it.

---

3   John Holahan, *et al.*, "The Sanders Single Payer Health Care Plan: The Effect on National Health Expenditures and Federal and State Spending," Urban Institute, May 9, 2016, https://www.urban.org/sites/default/files/publication/80486/200785-The-Sanders-Single-Payer-Health-Care-Plan.pdf; Jodi Liu and Christine Eibner, "National Health Spending Estimates Under Medicare for All," Rand Corporation, April 2019, https://www.rand.org/pubs/research_reports/RR3106.html.

4   Chris Jacobs, "Why Single Payer Wouldn't Get Americans More Health Care," *Federalist,* April 11, 2019, https://thefederalist.com/2019/04/11/single-payer-wouldnt-get-americans-health-care/.

5   See for instance Section 201(a) of H.R. 1384 and S. 1129, the Medicare for All Act of 2019.

REDUCING PHYSICIAN SUPPLY

The claim that moving to a single-payer system will reduce health-care costs comes down to a single premise: That doctors and hospitals will accept *less* pay to provide *more* health care to *more* patients.[6] If one disagrees with that premise—and logic suggests that most rational individuals would—then single payer will either lead to an explosion of health-care spending, or a reduction in the supply of care provided.

The current pricing system suggests the latter outcome will occur—namely, that doctors will decide to stop providing care, and may leave the profession entirely. Analysis from the office of the independent, non-partisan Medicare actuary explains why.

The actuary's office estimates that as of 2017, Medicare reimbursed physicians at an average of 75% of what private insurance pays them, and as of 2016, Medicaid paid physicians an average of 54% of private rates.[7] The actuary also believes that, under current law, Medicare payment rates will continue to fall over time, such that by 2092, Medicare will pay physicians only about 24%—less than one-quarter—of private insurance rates.[8]

---

6   Jacobs, "Sanders Supporters Admit."

7   John Shatto and Kent Clemens, "Projected Medicare Expenditures under an Illustrative Scenario with Alternative Payment Updates to Medicare Providers," Centers for Medicare and Medicaid Services Office of the Actuary memorandum, April 22, 2019, https://www.cms.gov/Research-Statistics-Data-and-Systems/Statistics-Trends-and-Reports/ReportsTrustFunds/Downloads/2019TRAlternativeScenario.pdf, p. 7.

8   Ibid.

Figure 2. Illustrative comparison of relative Medicare, Medicaid, and private health
insurance prices for physician services under current law

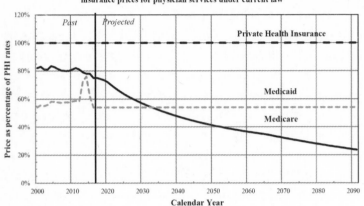

Centers for Medicare and Medicaid Services Office of the Actuary, April 2019.

The single-payer bills would cut physician payment significantly, by applying Medicare's current reimbursement levels to
the entire American population. Medicare does pay physicians
more than Medicaid does, meaning physicians who treat large
numbers of Medicaid patients might see no change in pay, or
even a slight increase.

But many more individuals hold private coverage—181 million with employer-sponsored coverage, compared to only about
72 million in Medicaid—meaning that most physicians will see
their pay cut under a single-payer system.[9] And remember: This

9   Edward Berchick, Emily Hood, and Jessica Barnett, "Health Insurance Coverage in
     the United States: 2017," Census Bureau Report P60-264, September 2018, https://
     www.census.gov/content/dam/Census/library/publications/2018/demo/p60-264.pdf,
     Table 1, Coverage Numbers and Rates by Type of Health Insurance: 2013, 2016, and
     2017, p. 4; Centers for Medicare and Medicaid Services, "December 2018 Medicaid
     and CHIP Enrollment Data Highlights," https://www.medicaid.gov/medicaid/
     program-information/medicaid-and-chip-enrollment-data/report-highlights/index.
     html.

pay cut will come at a time when demand for medical services will *increase*—due to the number of newly covered individuals, and the elimination of virtually all deductibles, co-payments, and other forms of cost-sharing.

Single-payer supporters argue that other nations' physicians earn much lower salaries, so the added spending on doctors in the United States represents "waste." Indeed, American physicians, particularly specialists, receive higher pay compared to many of their international peers. As of 2018, American physician salaries averaged $299,000, with the average specialist ($329,000) earning more than the average primary care physician ($223,000).[10] These salaries sound quite large to many Americans in absolute terms, and may look generous in the context of a 2011 survey that found doctors in six other developed countries earn anywhere from 35-86% of the salaries of their American peers.[11]

However, American physicians also carry very high loads of student debt needed to fund their education. In 2018, nearly three-quarters (72.3%) of graduating physicians said they used student loans to pay for medical school.[12] Of those who took on debt, the median medical school loan—that is, the 50th percentile—stood at $195,000.[13]

---

10   Leslie Kane, "Medscape Physician Compensation Report 2018," https://www.
      medscape.com/slideshow/2018-compensation-overview-6009667#2.

11   Miriam Laugesen and Sherry Glied, "Higher Fees Paid to U.S. Physicians
      Drive Higher Spending for Physician Services Compared to Other Countries,"
      Health Affairs, September 2011, https://www.healthaffairs.org/doi/full/10.1377/
      hlthaff.2010.0204.

12   Association of American Medical Colleges, "Medical School Graduation
      Questionnaire: 2018 All Schools Summary Report," July 2018, https://www.aamc.
      org/download/490454/data/2018gqallschoolssummaryreport.pdf, p. 44.

13   Ibid.

In other words, more than one-third (36.2%, or half of 72.3%) of graduating medical school students hold at least $200,000 in medical school debt, a sum that excludes loans from their undergraduate work and any other debt, such as a mortgage. Having taken on massive amounts of debt to join the medical profession, many doctors face burnout and fatigue once they do so.

Multiple surveys show high levels of frustration among physicians, in large part due to administrative hassles and bureaucracy. A 2018 survey found that nearly half (48%) of all physicians have considered leaving the profession due to their frustration.[14] While single-payer supporters blame private insurance companies for causing doctors' stress, doctors also believe that government policies (91%) contribute to rising health-care costs almost as much as they believe insurers do (95%).[15] Moreover, physicians' biggest problem with insurance companies—"overrid[ing] the professional judgement of physicians"—would not disappear under a single-payer system. In fact, it would likely get worse.[16]

The increasing care the United States' aging population needs, coupled with the retiring wave of doctors in the Baby Boom generation, means the nation's health system already faces a major physician shortage. Over the course of the next decade—between now and 2030—the United States faces an

---

14   Alliance for the Adoption of Innovations of Medicine, "Putting Profits Before Patients: Provider Perspectives on Health Insurance Barriers that Harm Patients," October 2018, https://aimedalliance.org/wp-content/uploads/2018/10/Aimed-Alliance-Primary-Care-Survey-Report.pdf, p. 18.

15   Ibid., p. 10.

16   Ibid., p. 11.

estimated shortfall of up to 121,300 physicians nationwide.[17] With the supply of available physicians already not meeting expected demand, single payer would cause demand for health care to explode, even as it constricts physicians' availability.

Single payer would exacerbate the forthcoming doctor shortage, reducing the available supply of care by driving physicians out of medicine. For doctors approaching retirement, the rapid changes envisioned by a new system, coupled with the steep pay cuts, would encourage them to hang up their proverbial spurs early. For mid-career physicians, the thought of performing more work for less pay could prompt them to leave the profession. And the prospect of permanently lower wages and high student debt could discourage some interested students from ever entering medical school.

Liberals like to believe that physicians will not respond to changing incentives, but low reimbursements have consequences on patients that single-payer supporters find highly inconvenient. Consider this article from a small newspaper from more than two decades ago:

> Dr. Judith Steinberg told her patients in a letter that Community Health Plan/Kaiser Permanente has cut payments to her practice while raising rates to its insured. The decision by Steinberg's group practice means several hundred patients in CHP's commercial and its "Access Plus" Medicaid plan will be obliged to either switch doctors or

---

17   IHS Markit, "The Complexities of Physician Supply and Demand: Projections from 2016 to 2030," Report for the American Association of Medical Colleges, March 2018, https://aamc-black.global.ssl.fastly.net/production/media/filer_public/85/ d7/85d7b689-f417-4ef0-97fb-ecc129836829/aamc_2018_workforce_projections_ update_april_11_2018.pdf.

switch insurers. The practice is the only CHP primary care provider in Shelburne.[18]

The article sounds innocuous enough, until one finds out the identity of Steinberg's husband: Gov. Howard Dean, like Sanders, a Vermont resident and a very public supporter of single-payer health care. To put it another way, Dean's wife dropped out of Vermont's largest Medicaid managed care plan because of its incredibly low reimbursement rates *while Dean was governor*, and in charge of the Medicaid program. That fact should quite literally bring home to single-payer supporters like Dean and Sanders that doctors could leave the profession in droves should this socialistic scheme come to fruition.

If patients have an insurance card, but no access to medical professionals who will treat them, their "coverage" will prove meaningless. One former head of a state Medicaid program—which in many states provides notoriously stingy payment rates to doctors—called a Medicaid card a "hunting license [that gives patients] a chance to go try to find a doctor" who will see them.[19] By encouraging doctors to leave the profession, single payer could leave most Americans with nothing more than a hunting license for medical care.

GLOBAL BUDGETS ENCOURAGE HOSPITALS TO CUT CORNERS
The Senate's single-payer bill would apply the existing Medicare

---

18   Associated Press, "Governor's Wife Cuts Ties with HMO," *Rutland (VT) Herald,* May 17, 1998.

19   Comments by DeAnn Friedholm at "Affordability and Health Reform: If We Mandate, Will They (And Can They) Pay?" Alliance for Health Reform briefing, November 20, 2009, http://www.allhealth.org/wp-content/uploads/2016/12/TranscriptFINAL-1685.pdf, p. 40.

fee schedule to hospitals as well as physicians.[20] As with the physician analysis above, applying Medicare reimbursement levels to all hospital patients would devastate facilities' finances. As we have seen, one study found that such a proposal would, for a hypothetical small hospital system, lead to a $330 million cut in revenues each year, and reduce margins from a surplus of 2.3% to a loss of 22.1%.[21]

However, the House's most recent version of single-payer legislation proposed a new way of paying hospitals, and a new way for the federal government to stint on patient care.

Under the House legislation, hospitals, along with groups of doctors who elect to opt in to the new system, would receive quarterly, lump-sum reimbursements as "payment in full for all operating expenses for items and services furnished under this Act, whether inpatient or outpatient."[22] The House bill requires each regional director for the new single-payer system to "negotiate" these quarterly payment amounts with hospital providers, based on the following payment factors:

1. "The historical volume of services provided for each item and services in the previous three-year period";

2. "The actual expenditures of such provider," as reported on hospital cost reports, when compared to expenses by other hospitals in the region and "normative payment rates established under comparative payment systems";

---

20 Section 611(a) of S. 1129.

21 Jeff Goldsmith, Jeff Leibach, and Kurt Eicher, "Medicare Expansion: A Preliminary Analysis of Hospital Financial Impacts," Navigant Consulting, March 2019, https://www.navigant.com/-/media/www/site/insights/healthcare/2019/medicare-expansion-analysis.pdf.

22 Section 611(a)(1) of H.R. 1384.

3. "Projected changes in the volume and type of items and services to be furnished";

4. "Wages for employees, including any necessary increases to ensure the optimal staffing levels for physicians and other health care workers";

5. "The provider's maximum capacity to provide items and services";

6. "Education and prevention programs";

7. "Permissible adjustment to the provider's operating budget due to factors such as" increasing health care access, eliminating disparities, responding to epidemics, and promoting new innovations; and

8. "Any other factor determined appropriate by the Secretary" of Health and Human Services (HHS).[23]

The regional directors will, after considering the factors above, determine the level of hospitals' lump-sum quarterly payments. Because the government system will cover practically all services, and because any hospital that accepts payments from the government system cannot contract with patients outside of the government system, the regional director's assessment will, for all intents and purposes, set hospitals' operating budgets each quarter.[24]

The process envisioned under the House bill provides tremendous authority to the regional directors, and to HHS as a

---

23 Section 611(b)(2) of H.R. 1384.

24 Section 301(b)(1) of H.R. 1384.

whole. The bill allows for the HHS secretary to set the number of regions and appoint the regional directors.[25] While the current head of the Centers for Medicare and Medicaid Services (CMS) must receive Senate confirmation, the bill denies the Senate any ability to provide "advice and consent" over the regional directors—even though these officials would effectively set the budgets for all the hospitals in their assigned areas.[26] Nor does the bill provide any ability for hospitals to appeal the regional director's determination, should a hospital consider their quarterly payment amounts inaccurate or insufficient.

Supporters of single payer would argue that providing hospitals with global payments will encourage efficiencies, by requiring them to stick within a defined budget. But the idea that the federal government can set accurate budgets for thousands of hospitals nationwide seems fanciful at best, and dangerous at worst. If the federal government does not set accurate budget levels, and some hospitals end up under-funded, they will likely have to deny patients care. As the next chapter will explain in greater detail, paltry global budget payments in Great Britain have resulted in "severe financial strains" for that country's National Health Service, with tens of thousands of operations canceled and massive delays, even for emergency care.[27]

Two provisions in the House bill suggest that its authors intend to save costs by restricting the supply of care. In discussing

---

25   Section 403 of H.R. 1384.

26   Section 403(b)(1) of H.R. 1384.

27   Congressional Budget Office, "Key Design Components and Considerations for Establishing a Single Payer Health Care System," May 1, 2019, https://www.cbo.gov/system/files/2019-05/55150-singlepayer.pdf, p. 26.

payments to hospitals, the House bill prohibits hospitals from using "operating expenses and funds" to finance "a capital project funded by charitable donations," without the express approval of the regional director.[28] In other words, hospitals may not use federal dollars to operate new parts of the hospital *that they build and pay for themselves*—using charitable contributions rather than capital expenses provided by the government system. This restriction indicates how much single-payer proponents want to ration health care by restricting its supply.

Surprisingly, the House's single-payer bill also concedes that the new system will not lead to better-quality care. The bill prohibits HHS from "utiliz[ing] any quality metrics or standards for the purposes of establishing provider payment methodologies...under this title."[29] Think about that for a moment: The bill actually prohibits the federal government from paying good doctors and hospitals more than bad ones.

Mind you, conservatives might argue that the government cannot effectively determine the "best" care, and that those decisions belong in the hands of patients. But they would agree that "good" doctors and hospitals, however defined, should receive more pay than bad ones. The House single-payer bill explicitly rejects that principle, making its other provisions on quality standards effectively moot. And because quality metrics do not matter to hospitals' pay, the global budgets will give them every incentive to pinch pennies by denying care.

---

28   Section 614(c)(4) of H.R. 1384.

29   Section 614(f) of H.R. 1384.

DENYING PATIENTS "COSTLY" CARE

Among the biggest proponents of the global budgets included in the House's single-payer bill: Donald Berwick, administrator at CMS following the passage of Obamacare. Berwick—infamous for his comments about "rationing with our eyes open"—also advocated for capping total spending on health care.[30] In journal articles, he promoted "global caps on health care spending," ideally through a single-payer system.[31]

Berwick's writings provide rich insights into the thinking of his fellow single-payer proponents. He envisions a centralized system run by technocrats, whom he believes will make efficient decisions about where and how to allocate resources. It sounds well and good until the implications of this type of system become apparent.

First, Berwick would sharply limit the supply of health care available—which, in his mind, represents perhaps the only way to control rising costs. In 1993, he wrote that most cities "should reduce the number of centers engaging in cardiac surgery, high-risk obstetrics, neonatal intensive care, organ transplantation, tertiary cancer care, high-level trauma care, and high-technology imaging."[32]

Most people would find the idea of shutting down cancer

30 "Rethinking Comparative Effectiveness Research," An Interview with Dr. Donald Berwick, *Biotechnology Healthcare,* June 2009, http://www.ncbi.nlm.nih.gov/pmc/articles/PMC2799075/pdf/bth06_2p035.pdf.

31 Donald Berwick, Thomas Nolan, and John Whittington, "The Triple Aim: Care, Health, and Cost," *Health Affairs,* May/June 2008, https://www.healthaffairs.org/doi/pdf/10.1377/hlthaff.27.3.759.

32 Donald M. Berwick, "Buckling Down to Change," speech to 5th annual National Forum on Quality Improvement in Health Care, December 1993, in Berwick, *Escape Fire: Designs for the Future of Health Care* (Jossey-Bass, 2004), pp. 28-29.

centers and neonatal intensive care units offensive and scary, in case they or a loved one might need them. For instance, had policy-makers followed Berwick's advice a quarter-century ago, and shut down neonatal intensive care units, babies born with opioid withdrawal symptoms during our nation's current crisis with that drug might have faced even tougher odds. But Berwick apparently believes that he and his fellow technocrats can better manage care for the American people than doctors and patients can.

Of course, limiting the supply of health care also implies that government bureaucrats can determine the "correct" amount of care to provide—no more, no less. Berwick believes passionately in such an outcome: "I want to see that in the city of San Diego or Seattle there are exactly as many MRI units as needed when operating at full capacity. Not less and not more."[33] Over and above the important question of whether the government *should* have the power to determine the "correct" number of MRI units in San Diego or Seattle, it's not at all clear that government could determine that number with any level of accuracy or consistency.

Second, Berwick believes that, in at least some cases, doctors should fail to treat their individual patients' needs if doing so would harm the "collective good." In 1999, he and several colleagues signed a declaration calling on their fellow physicians not to "manipulate"—their exact words—the system to help individual patients:

> Limited resources require decisions about who will have access to care and the extent of their coverage. The complexity

---

33   "QMHC Interview: Donald M. Berwick, MD," *Quality Management in Health Care* (Fall 1993): 76.

and cost of healthcare delivery systems may set up a tension between what is good for the society as a whole and what is best for an individual patient....Those working in health care delivery may be faced with situations in which it seems that the best course is to manipulate the flawed system for the benefit of a specific patient or segment of the population, rather than to work to improve the delivery of care for all. Such manipulation produces more flaws, and the downward spiral continues.[34]

By specifically using the term "manipulate" to refer to doctors who try to help their individual patients, Berwick makes clear his view that, with costly care, individuals must sacrifice their wishes and desires to the will of the collective—which to liberals means the will of the government.

The president for whom Berwick worked has also acknowledged that government may need to limit access to costly medical treatments. Barack Obama waited until after Congress had enacted Obamacare before nominating the controversial Berwick to the CMS administrator post.[35] But in a 2009 interview with the *New York Times*, Obama, while acknowledging the human costs of such policies, implied that at some point, government would have to limit access to treatments:

The chronically ill and those toward the end of their lives are accounting for potentially 80 percent of the total health care

---

34   Richard Smith, Howard Hiatt, and Donald Berwick, "A Shared Statement of Ethical Principles," *BMJ*, January 23, 1999, https://www.ncbi.nlm.nih.gov/pmc/articles/PMC1114728/.

35   Berwick's nomination still proved so contentious that Democrats refused to bring him up for a confirmation vote, despite controlling 59 seats in the Senate.

bill out here....There is going to have to be a conversation that is guided by doctors, scientists, ethicists. And then there is going to have to be a very difficult democratic conversation that takes place.[36]

Approximately two months after that interview, at a televised event on health care held at the White House, Obama spoke with Jean Sturm, the daughter of a patient who received a pacemaker at age 100. When Sturm asked Obama about how he might determine access to care for the elderly, Obama first discussed how "we as a culture and as a society [should start] to make better decisions."

But then he talked about "waste in the system," culminating in the following: "We can let doctors know and your mom know that, you know what? Maybe this isn't going to help. Maybe you're better off not having the surgery, but taking the painkiller."[37]

Other appointees in the Obama administration came up with their own theories for making difficult decisions about access to treatments. In 2009, Zeke Emanuel—brother of Rahm, and an advisor in the Office of Management and Budget during the debate on Obamacare—wrote an article entitled "Principles for Allocation of Scarce Medical Interventions," that included the following chart demonstrating his theory:

---

36   David Leonhardt, "After the Great Recession," *New York Times,* April 28, 2009, https://www.nytimes.com/2009/05/03/magazine/03Obama-t.html.

37   "Obama's Health Future," *Wall Street Journal,* June 29, 2009, https://www.wsj.com/articles/SB124597492337757443; video of the exchange available at https://www.youtube.com/watch?v=U-dQfb8WQvo.

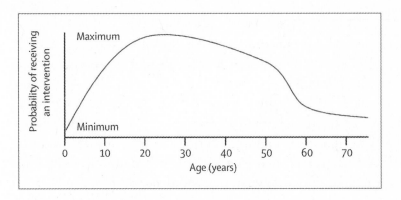

Zeke Emanuel et al., The Lancet, January 2009. Reprinted with permission.

If a picture is worth a thousand words, then this chart certainly speaks volumes.[38]

In that same article, Emanuel articulated the principles behind the same debate Berwick and Obama engaged in, on how to allocate scarce medical resources:

> Adolescents have received substantial education and parental care, investments that will be wasted without a complete life. Infants, by contrast, have not yet received these investments.... The complete lives system discriminates against older people.... [However,] age, like income, is a "non-medical criterion" inappropriate for allocation of medical resources.

Emanuel admitted that decisions to allocate scarce medical resources will, almost by definition, discriminate against the most vulnerable in society—the very young and the very old.

---

38 Govind Persad, Alan Wertheimer, and Ezekiel Emanuel, "Principles for Allocation of Scarce Medical Interventions," *Lancet,* January 31, 2009, https://www.scribd.com/document/18280675/Principles-for-Allocation-of-Scarce-Medical-Interventions.

If those quotes do not give one pause, consider another quote by Zeke Emanuel, this one from a 1996 work: "[Health care] services provided to individuals who are irreversibly prevented from being or becoming participating citizens are not basic and should not be guaranteed. An obvious example is not guaranteeing health services to patients with dementia."[39] When that quote resurfaced during the debate on Obamacare in 2009, Emanuel attempted to claim he had never actually advocated for this position, but he wrote the words nonetheless.[40]

Unfortunately, as Sturm recognized during the June 2009 town hall with President Obama, setting hard-and-fast rules about access to care—as she termed it, "a medical cut-off at a certain age"—means someone almost certainly will suffer in the exchange. Even if the federal government can make "good" (i.e., medically accurate) decisions about what care to provide, and not provide, the *average* patient, a single patient by definition is not average.

In many cases, for example, drug and device manufacturers find it difficult to test their products for pediatric use because developing bodies process drugs differently than adults do, and because so few young people need to use devices like pacemakers.[41] Likewise, many clinical trials have historically under-represented key populations, such as women, particularly pregnant

---

39   Ezekiel Emanuel, "Where Civic Republicanism and Deliberative Democracy Meet," *Hastings Center Report,* November/December 1996, https://www.jstor.org/stable/3528746.

40   D'Angelo Gore, "Deadly Doctor?" FactCheck.Org, August 14, 2009, https://www.factcheck.org/2009/08/deadly-doctor/.

41   Chris Jacobs, "Dad of Sick Child Explains Why Single Payer Always Leads to Rationing," *Federalist,* March 6, 2009, http://thefederalist.com/2019/03/06/dad-sick-child-explains-single-payer-always-leads-rationing/.

women, and racial minorities. Genomic trials continue to under-represent such patients today.[42] A drug or treatment that works poorly for most of the population could work incredibly well for certain individuals, or important sub-populations—but only if researchers have that information readily available and are willing to put it into practice.

If bureaucrats make coverage decisions based on the response of the "average" patient, then populations under-represented in research could especially suffer.

Creating blanket, one-size-fits-all coverage rules would impede access to these treatments for those who need, or could benefit from, them most. As with most well-intentioned government interventions, the people the Left claims they most want to help—vulnerable populations, with little access to clinical trials, and few resources to pay for costly treatments out of their own pockets—may well end up suffering the greatest harm.

UNDERMINING THE CULTURE OF LIFE

In addition to restricting care for vulnerable patients with expensive health conditions, single payer also jeopardizes the rights of the unborn. Both the House and Senate bills include

---

42   Katherine Liu and Natalie Dipietro Mager, "Women's Involvement in Clinical Trials: Historical Perspective and Future Implications," *Pharmacy Practice,* January-March 2016, https://www.ncbi.nlm.nih.gov/pmc/articles/PMC4800017/; "Report of the Task Force on Research Specific to Pregnant Women and Lactating Women," September 2018, https://www.nichd.nih.gov/sites/default/files/2018-09/PRGLAC_Report.pdf; Caroline Chen and Riley Wong, "Black Patients Miss Out on Promising Cancer Drugs," *ProPublica,* September 19, 2018, https://www.propublica.org/article/black-patients-miss-out-on-promising-cancer-drugs; Jonathan Lambert, "Human Genomics Research Has a Diversity Problem," NPR, March 21, 2019, https://www.npr.org/sections/health-shots/2019/03/21/705460986/human-genomics-research-has-a-diversity-problem.

a provision stating that "any other provision of law in effect on the date of enactment of this Act restricting the use of federal funds for any reproductive health service shall not apply" to the single-payer system.[43]

This provision would effectively ensure that the Hyde Amendment's restrictions on taxpayer funding of abortion would not apply to the single-payer system. Former Congressman Henry Hyde (R-IL) helped enact the eponymous provision in 1976; Congress has included the language in its annual spending bills every year since then. In its current form, the Hyde Amendment prevents taxpayer funding of abortion, except in cases of rape, incest, or to save the life of the mother.[44]

Just a few years ago, Democrats said they wanted to ensure no taxpayer dollars funded abortion coverage. In his address to Congress in September 2009, Obama claimed that "under our plan, no federal dollars will be used to fund abortions."[45] Two months later, 64 Democratic members of Congress voted to put Obama's claim into practice, supporting an amendment offered by Rep. Bart Stupak (D-MI) that would have prevented any Obamacare insurance plan from offering coverage for elective abortions—that is, abortions outside the Hyde Amendment's three stated exceptions (rape, incest, and to save the life of the mother).[46]

Unfortunately, the version of Obamacare enacted into

---

43 Section 701(b)(3) of H.R. 1384 and S. 1129.

44 Jon Shimabukuro, "Abortion: Judicial History and Legislative Response," Congressional Research Service Report RL33467, December 7, 2018, https://fas.org/sgp/crs/misc/RL33467.pdf.

45 Barack Obama, Speech to a Joint Session of Congress, September 9, 2009, https://www.cbsnews.com/news/transcript-obamas-health-care-speech/.

46 House Amendment 509 to H.R. 3962 (111th Congress); House Roll Call Vote 884 of 2009, http://clerk.house.gov/evs/2009/roll884.xml.

law did not include the Stupak amendment's life protections. Instead, Democrats constructed a segregation mechanism, whereby taxpayer dollars could still flow to insurance plans that cover abortion, so long as insurers could supposedly keep the abortion dollars "separate."[47] Pro-life groups rightly exposed this mechanism as an accounting gimmick, due to money's inherent fungibility.[48] Government auditors also said the Obama administration failed to implement even these minimal restrictions on abortion funding.[49]

But at least Democrats felt the need to claim they opposed taxpayer funding of abortion, even if their proposals did not fulfill their rhetoric. No more. The left wing of the party is now pushing for a vote to abolish the Hyde Amendment, to allow for taxpayer funding of abortion at any time in a pregnancy and for any reason.[50]

The language in the single-payer bill, which would prevent the Hyde Amendment's restrictions from applying to the new government program, merely reflects the party's movement ever leftward. It also would allow abortion for many weeks during which the unborn child could be saved through a C-section, an

---

47   Section 1303(b)(2) of the Patient Protection and Affordable Care Act, P.L. 111-148, codified at 42 U.S.C. 18023(b)(2).

48   Arina Grossu, "Abortion Funding and Obamacare," Family Research Council Issue Analysis IS14F01, September 2016, https://downloads.frc.org/EF/EF14F35.pdf.

49   Government Accountability Office, "Coverage of Non-Excepted Abortion Services by Qualified Health Plans," Report GAO-13-742R, September 15, 2014, https://www.gao.gov/assets/670/665800.pdf.

50   H.R. 1692 and S. 758, Equal Access to Abortion Coverage in Health Insurance Act; Jessie Hellmann, "House Dems to Push Pelosi for Vote on Bill That Would Allow Federal Funding of Abortion," *The Hill,* March 12, 2019, https://thehill.com/policy/healthcare/433700-house-dems-to-push-pelosi-for-vote-on-bill-that-would-allow-federal-funding.

allowance large and bipartisan majorities of Americans oppose.

Likewise, nothing in either the House or the Senate bills prohibits the federal government, and HHS, from paying for euthanasia through the single-payer program. With eight states now having authorized "aid in dying," a future administration could easily rule that such means constitute "medically... appropriate" action for "treatment...of a health condition."[51]

In fact, both bills require HHS to use "new information from medical research" and "other relevant developments in health science" to update the list of covered benefits.[52] If more states authorize euthanasia, the case for paying for it through single-payer would only grow, especially as a cost-saving measure given the massive costs of end-of-life care.

A culture that encourages euthanasia places a premium on the collective—as determined by government bureaucrats—over preserving each and every life, no matter how vulnerable, and especially when vulnerable. In this context, Berwick's comments prove most revealing, as they illustrate how liberals believe physicians should not "manipulate" the system to ensure a single specific patient benefits.

That philosophy explains how single-payer systems contain costs: by limiting the supply of care in general, and denying access to costly care in particular. An examination of single-payer systems overseas demonstrates how patients often wait—and wait, and wait some more—for care, and in some cases never receive it at all.

---

51   Sam Sutton, "Murphy Signs Aid in Dying Bill into Law," *Politico* April 12, 2019, https://www.politico.com/states/new-jersey/story/2019/04/12/murphy-signs-aid-in-dying-bill-into-law-966815; Section 201(a) of H.R. 1384 and S. 1129.

52   Section 201(b) of H.R. 1384 and S. 1129.

7

THE PAIN OTHER SINGLE-PAYER SYSTEMS INFLICT

KEY POINTS

- Single-payer systems have demonstrated records of denying patients access to care to contain costs.

- Patients in Canada and Britain—two countries with single-payer health systems—have far less access to specialized yet costly treatments like MRI machines and CT scans than do patients in the United States.

- In Canada, patients needing specialist care must wait an average of five months from an initial referral until starting treatment; waiting times average nearly ten months for orthopedic surgery.

- In Britain, the National Institute of Health and Care Excellence (NICE) restricts access to drugs and treatments not deemed cost effective. Single-payer legislation could bring similar practices to the United States.

- The Veterans Health Administration scandal illustrated the problems inherent in single-payer systems: Lack of funding means the supply of health care cannot meet demand, resulting in waiting times—and efforts by bureaucrats to conceal those waiting times.

- Because single-payer legislation would make private insurance "unlawful," American patients, unlike those in Canada and Great Britain, may have little recourse should the federal government deny them access to costly care.

Single-payer supporters portray socialized medicine as a utopia in which everyone gets all the health care he or she needs, free of charge. The facts suggest otherwise. In reality, single-payer systems have a proven track record of denying patients prompt access to treatment, and providing low-quality care.

In Canada, health officials keep costs low by restricting the supply of care, forcing people to wait months for treatment. Even Canada's highest court has criticized its health system, noting that access to a waiting list does not represent access to care.

In Great Britain, chronic underfunding has created repeated crises in hospitals, as lack of capacity means patients wait for care. Moreover, Britain's National Health Service (NHS) restricts access to drugs not deemed cost-effective by government bureaucrats, denying British patients life-saving treatments available in other countries.

And who can forget that right here in the United States,

our veterans' health system suffered a scandal in which patients who had survived the battlefield in the service of their country died when they came home—because the government could not provide them prompt access to care? The way Department of Veterans Affairs officials manipulated patient charts to meet government waiting list targets illuminates what a single-payer system would bring to all Americans.

At least in the case of Canada, Britain, and the VA, patients have the option to "go private"—to purchase private insurance, or obtain care at facilities run outside the government system. But if single-payer legislation makes private health insurance in the United States "unlawful," patients may not even have those other options to obtain prompt care. The end result could resemble The Eagles' proverbial "Hotel California," one in which "You can check out any time you like—but you can never leave."

CANADA'S QUEUES: HEALTH CARE BY WAITING

In 2017, Canada spent less than half the amount the United States did on health care per person: $6,082 versus $12,865.[1] Canada spent less on health care than the United States as a percentage of the country's Gross Domestic Product (GDP), but also had a smaller GDP per person than the United States, giving Canadians less to spend overall.[2]

Because it spends less money on health care than the United States, the Canadian system results in less care to give.

---

1   Canadian Institute for Health Information, "How Canada Compares Internationally: A Health Spending Perspective, 2018," November 20, 2018, https://www.cihi.ca/sites/default/files/document/nhex-2018-international-chartbook-en-web.pptx.

2   Ibid.

Organization for Economic Cooperation and Development (OECD) statistics demonstrate that, expressed as totals per million inhabitants, Canadians cannot access care as readily as Americans do:

- Canadians have less than one-third as many magnetic resonance imaging (MRI) machines (9.97) as Americans (37.56);

- Canadians have less than half as many computed tomography (CT) scanners (15.28) than Americans (42.64);

- Canadians have one-third the number of mammography machines (18.34) as Americans (55.45);

- Canadians have one-fourth the number of radiotherapy machines (2.94) as Americans (11.92); and

- Canadians also have less access to hospital beds per 1,000 inhabitants (2.55) than do Americans (2.8).[3]

Because Canada's government limits the care available to maintain lower levels of spending, patients must often wait to access treatment.

Canada's health system has become defined by a "queuing culture," in which patients cannot receive care when they need it. The Fraser Institute, a Vancouver-based think tank, has conducted annual surveys of wait times in Canada's health system. The results from Fraser's 2018 survey may astonish Americans:

---

3   Organization for Economic Cooperation and Development, "OECD Health Statistics," https://data.oecd.org/healtheqt/hospital-beds.htm.

- Patients waited an average of 8.7 weeks, or two months, to see a specialist after a referral from a general practitioner (GP);

- After waiting two months to see a specialist, patients waited another 11 weeks, or nearly three months, to start their course of treatment;

- Since the Fraser Institute started its survey in 1993, the average waiting time from GP referral to the start of treatment has increased by 113%, from 9.3 weeks to 19.8 weeks;

- In the worst province of New Brunswick, patients waited an average of 45 weeks—or about 11 months—from GP referral to the start of treatment;

- Patients waited the longest time—39 weeks, or nearly 10 months—for orthopedic surgery;

- Patients waited an average of 4.3 weeks for a CT scan, 10.6 weeks for an MRI, and 3.9 weeks for an ultrasound; and

- A total of 1,082,541 patients in Canada, or 2.9% of the population, were waiting for treatment.[4]

Most Americans would find delays of both this length and magnitude unacceptable. If 2.9% of the population had to wait for access to treatment in a country the size of the United States, that would equate to approximately 9.4 million Americans

---

4   Bacchus Barua, David Jacques, and Antonia Collyer, "Waiting Your Turn: Wait Times for Health Care in Canada, 2018 Report," Fraser Institute, December 4, 2018, https://www.fraserinstitute.org/sites/default/files/waiting-your-turn-2018.pdf.

waiting for access to health care—greater than the populations of Los Angeles, Chicago, and Houston *combined*.[5]

Waiting for care has monetary and emotional, to say nothing of physical, costs. The Fraser Institute attempted to quantify the value of these health care queues on the Canadian economy. Their research concluded that waiting lists cost Canadians $2.1 billion in reduced economic output during working hours, and a total of $6.3 billion including their non-working hours.[6] Moreover, because this Fraser study only incorporated waiting times after patients saw a specialist, it significantly underestimated the effects of health-care queues on Canadian patients, most of whom must wait months to see a specialist in the first place.

Some individuals might think that, while Canadians must wait for months to receive specialist care, at least Canada provides prompt access to primary care. Think again. A 2016 survey of patients in 11 countries, including the United States, found that Canada also had comparatively poor access to primary care:

- The lowest percentage of patients (43%) who said they could get an appointment the same day or the next day to see a doctor or nurse;

---

5   Edward Berchick, Emily Hood, and Jessica Barnett, "Health Insurance Coverage in the United States: 2017," Census Bureau Report P60-264, September 2018, https://www.census.gov/content/dam/Census/library/publications/2018/demo/p60-264.pdf, Table 1, Coverage Numbers and Rates by Type of Health Insurance: 2013, 2016, and 2017, p. 4.

6   Bacchus Barua and David Jaques, "The Private Cost of Public Queues for Medically Necessary Care, 2019," Fraser Institute, March 28, 2019, https://www.fraserinstitute.org/sites/default/files/private-cost-public-queues-medically-necessary-care-2019.pdf.

- The second-lowest percentage of patients (34%) who said it was easy to receive after-hours care without going to the emergency room;

- The lowest percentage of patients (59%) who said they often or always receive an answer the same day when calling the doctor's office about a medical issue;

- The highest percentage of patients (41%) using the emergency room; and

- The highest percentage of patients (29%) waiting four or more hours in the emergency room.[7]

Canada's health-care system provides such poor access to care that between 217,500 and 323,700 patients—nearly 1% of Canada's population—left the country for care in 2017, choosing to pay out-of-pocket rather than suffer seemingly perpetual waits for "free" treatment.[8] With poor access to both specialists and primary care, Canada's single-payer system provides a grim picture of the future Americans might soon face.

Canada's health system provides such poor access to care that the nation's Supreme Court issued a landmark ruling against it. In 2005, the court heard a case in which George Zeliotis, a Canadian who had struggled to receive access to care,

---

7   Canadian Institute for Health Information, "How Canada Compares: Results from the Commonwealth Fund's 2016 National Health Policy Survey of Adults in 11 Countries," February 16, 2017, https://www.cihi.ca/sites/default/files/document/commonwealth-fund-2016-chartbook-en-web-rev.pptx.

8   Colin Craig, "Policy Brief: The Flight of the Sick," Second Street, March 2019, https://www.secondstreet.org/wp-content/uploads/2019/03/Policy-Brief-Flight-of-the-Sick.pdf.

and Jacques Chaoulli, a physician rejected for a license to open an independent hospital, challenged the province of Quebec's ban on private health insurance—the same kind of prohibition included in the House and Senate single-payer bills. The court, noting that "access to a waiting list is not access to care," struck down Quebec's ban on private coverage.[9]

One line in particular from Canada's Supreme Court should warn single-payer supporters. The court found that

> Prohibiting health insurance that would permit ordinary Canadians to access health care, in circumstances where the government is failing to deliver health care in a reasonable manner, thereby increasing the risk of complications and death, interferes with life and security of the person.[10]

"Interfer[ing] with the life and security of the person" aptly describes the health-care system in Canada, and the restrictions single-payer supporters wish to export to the United States.

BRITISH RATIONING NOT SO NICE

Britain's government-run NHS suffers from many of the same shortcomings. As with the Canadian system, the NHS attempts to contain costs by limiting the available supply of care. Like Canada, the British system also compares poorly to the United State in access to MRI machines, CT scanners, and radiotherapy equipment.[11] Britain also provides fewer hospital beds per

---

9   *Chaoulli v. Quebec*, 2005 SCC 35.

10   Ibid.

11   Organization for Economic Cooperation and Development, "OECD Health Statistics." Data for mammography equipment were unavailable for the United Kingdom.

1,000 residents (2.58) than the United States does (2.8).[12]

The past several winters have exposed the NHS's capacity problems in stark light. Chronic under-funding, coupled with the onset of influenza season, resulted in escalating crises within the NHS—so much so that the first four days of 2018 saw more mentions of the word "NHS" with the words "winter crisis" than for the entire years 2003 through 2009 combined.[13] When costs rise due to an aging population and greater use of services, but taxpayer spending fails to keep pace, people must wait longer for services. The percentage of Britons spending more than four hours in the emergency room rose appreciably during the last decade, leading to bottlenecks throughout hospital systems.[14]

In January 2018, the combination of under-funding and a bad flu season stretched Britain's NHS to the breaking point. Prime Minister Theresa May ended up offering apologies to British patients for the conditions they faced:

- Up to 55,000 operations postponed

- An emergency room doctor who felt the need publicly to apologize to patients for "Third World conditions of the department due to overcrowding"

- Advisories that patients should not go to the emergency room "unless they are very seriously ill"

---

12 Ibid.

13 Harry Carr, "Why Is There Always a Winter Crisis in the NHS?" *Sky News,* January 4, 2018, https://news.sky.com/story/why-is-there-always-a-winter-crisis-in-the-nhs-11195502.

14 Ibid.

- Up to two dozen ambulances parked outside a hospital, "with an average of 10 to 14 vehicles waiting to drop off patients throughout the day," because the hospitals had no place to put the incoming patients[15]

While the canceled operations and overcrowding drove headlines in the moment, a critical analysis found that the problems leading to the "crisis" appeared more structural.[16] The Congressional Budget Office's May 2019 analysis hedged on many specifics regarding single payer, but it made crystal clear that the NHS has suffered from serious shortcomings in recent years. In CBO's estimation, those flaws came from under-funding caused by the global budget mechanism that the House's single-payer bill would bring to the United States:

> In England, the global budget is allocated to approximately 200 local organizations that are responsible for paying for health care. Since 2010, the global budget in England has grown by about 1 percent annually in real (inflation-adjusted) terms, compared with an average real growth of about 4 percent previously. The relatively slow growth in the global

---

15 Sophie Borland, Claire Duffin, and James Tozer, "Winter Crisis Cripples the NHS: 55,000 Operations Are Postponed, Patients Are to Be Put on Mixed Wards, and Senior Doctors Will Man Doors at A&E Wards to Turn Away Non-Urgent Cases," *Daily Mail,* January 3, 2018, https://www.dailymail.co.uk/news/article-5229733/Thousands-NHS-operations-cancelled-winter.html#ixzz537tRpXfJ; Benjamin Kentish, "NHS Winter Crisis: Theresa May Apologizes to Patients for Thousands of Cancelled Operations," *Independent* (UK), January 4, 2018, https://www.independent.co.uk/news/uk/politics/theresa-may-nhs-crisis-winter-apology-patients-cancelled-operations-latest-updates-a8141591.html.

16 Siva Anandaciva, "A&E Performance Reaches a New Low," *The King's Fund,* January 12, 2018, https://www.kingsfund.org.uk/blog/2018/01/ae-performance-reaches-new-low.

budget since 2010 has created severe financial strains on the health care system. Provider payment rates have been reduced, many providers have incurred financial deficits, and wait times for receiving care have increased.[17]

With hospitals running at near 95% capacity heading into the peak influenza period in 2018—approximately 10 percentage points above NHS targets—most facilities could barely cope with their regular patient populations and workloads.[18] With very little margin for error or "surge capacity," any problem in the health system, let alone an aggressive strain of the flu, would, and did, stretch the NHS beyond its limits.

Britain's NHS doesn't just attempt to save costs by restricting the supply of hospital care provided. It also restricts access to pharmaceutical treatments. The country's National Institute of Health and Care Excellence has what some might consider an Orwellian acronym, because few find its decisions very NICE. In Britain, the NHS blocks patients from accessing treatments the institute doesn't deem cost-effective.

Originally founded as the National Institute for Clinical Excellence in 1999, NICE establishes thresholds above which the NHS generally will not cover expensive treatments. It does so by using Quality-Adjusted Life Years (QALYs)—its estimation of the value of a year of life in perfect health. To use a crude example, if a drug extends a life by three months, and one

---

17   Section 611 of H.R. 1384, the Medicare for All Act of 2019; Congressional Budget Office, "Key Design Components and Considerations for Establishing a Single Payer Health Care System," May 1, 2019, https://www.cbo.gov/system/files/2019-05/55150-singlepayer.pdf, p. 26.

18   Anandaciva, "A&E Performance Reaches a New Low."

values a year of life at \$100,000, the drug would have a QALY of \$25,000 (\$100,000 times one-fourth of a year). NICE's more granular analyses also consider the quality of life extended by a particular drug or treatment.

While NICE does not have hard-and-fast rules for drugs' cost-effectiveness, it scrutinizes drugs with a high cost per QALY:

> As a treatment approaches a cost of £20,000 [about \$26,000-\$27,000 at 2019 exchange rates] per QALY gained over existing best practice, NICE will scrutinize it closely. It will consider how robust the analysis relating to its cost- and clinical-effectiveness is, how innovative the treatment is, and other factors. As the cost rises above £30,000 [about \$40,000] per QALY, NICE states that "an increasingly stronger case for supporting the technology as an effective use of NHS resources" is necessary.[19]

Advocates of this approach believe it helps to force pharmaceutical companies to lower the prices of their drugs, so they will meet NICE's thresholds. However, some drugs do not meet the thresholds, in which case local NHS trusts often will not cover the therapies.

Stories of the effects of rationing within Britain's NHS frequently feature in the country's media. In 2006 one general practitioner, Sarah Jarvis, wrote a firsthand account of her difficulty in caring for her patients, entitled "Sentenced to Death by NICE":

---

19   Nigel Edwards, Helen Crump, and Mark Dayan, "Rationing in the NHS," Nuffield Trust Policy Brief #2, February 2015, https://www.nuffieldtrust.org.uk/files/2017-01/rationing-in-the-nhs-web-final.pdf, p. 8.

I was left feeling furious and frustrated after a visit from a patient called Peter. He'd just had a serious heart attack and my job as a GP was to reduce his very high risk of having another. I knew what the latest research told me was the best way, but I had just basically been forbidden to use it by an official email from the Department of Health.[20]

She went on to explain that, while she initially supported NICE's creation, the organization had strayed from its original mission, and "served as a brake" on the introduction of new therapies.[21] Jarvis recounted how one committee to evaluate a cancer therapy had health economists on its panel to estimate the drug's costs, but no cancer specialists to gauge its clinical impact.[22]

Jarvis also noted how NICE initially tried to restrict access to cholesterol-reducing statin drugs for seniors, despite a "wealth of evidence" proving their effectiveness. She wrote that she found it "hard to escape the conclusion that there is a bias against treating elderly people properly simply because…they are an increasing burden on the taxpayer."[23]

Despite these flaws in its research process, and the thousands of people denied access to care due to NICE research, some experts consider the organization a "success story" that is "internationally admired and copied."[24] In fact, one British

---

20 Sarah Jarvis, "Sentenced to Death by NICE," *Daily Mail,* November 27, 2006, https://www.dailymail.co.uk/health/article-419083/Sentenced-death-NICE.html.

21 Ibid.

22 Ibid.

23 Ibid.

24 Edwards, Crump, and Dayan, "Rationing in the NHS," pp. 8-9.

think tank called for the abolition of the Cancer Drugs Fund, created by the Conservative government in 2011 and designed to provide access to costly therapies NICE didn't deem cost-effective.[25] Other health-care analysts want to bring the NICE model of rationing to the United States.

Only a few weeks after President Obama told the *New York Times* in 2009 that he wanted to consult ethicists for a "difficult democratic conversation" about restricting access to costly treatments, one such ethicist wrote a lengthy essay in the *Times* supporting the use of cost effectiveness research in the United States.[26] The article, entitled "Why We Must Ration Health Care," said that the QALY "tells us to do what brings about the greatest health benefit," even though he admitted the approach "may then lead us to give priority to helping others who are not so badly off and whose conditions are less expensive to treat."[27] Ironically enough, however, this ethicist believed that Americans would allow government to ration health care in such a manner only if "the option of private health insurance remains available"—which it would not under the House and Senate single-payer bills.[28]

The U.S. single-payer bills would bring British-style rationing of health care to the United States, with only minor variations. One section of the House legislation includes the

---

25   Ibid., p. 10.

26   David Leonhardt, "After the Great Recession," *The New York Times* April 28, 2009, https://www.nytimes.com/2009/05/03/magazine/03Obama-t.html.

27   Peter Singer, "Why We Must Ration Health Care," *New York Times,* July 15, 2009, https://www.nytimes.com/2009/07/19/magazine/19healthcare-t.html.

28   Ibid.

following language regarding cost-effectiveness research:

> The use of Quality-Adjusted Life Years, Disability-Adjusted Life Years, or other similar mechanisms that discriminate against people with disabilities is prohibited for use in any value or cost-effectiveness assessments.[29]

This language, and the bill in general, do not prohibit cost-effectiveness research—quite the contrary, in fact. Other sections of the bill explicitly reference "cost effectiveness" research as one way to determine the value of physician-delivered services and prescription drugs.[30] The language described above merely prohibits "mechanisms that discriminate against people with disabilities," making cost effectiveness research that devalues other groups—for instance, the very young or the very old—perfectly permissible.

Moreover, the Senate bill includes no provision whatsoever blocking the use of QALYs.[31] When compared to its companion in the House, such an omission seems particularly noteworthy—an implicit yet deliberate admission that the single-payer system will use cost-effectiveness research to deny access to expensive treatments. As with many elements of government-run health care, this provision will most harm the most vulnerable—those without the means to purchase or access care on their own.

---

29   Section 501(b)(2) of H.R. 1384.

30   Sections 612(d) and 616(1)(A) of H.R. 1384.

31   Compare Sections 501(b)(2) and 612(d) of H.R. 1384 with Sections 501(b)(2) and 611 of S. 1129, the Medicare for All Act of 2019.

WORSE HEALTH OUTCOMES OVERSEAS

Denying patients costly treatments affects health outcomes, as overseas comparisons demonstrate. For instance, one study examining differences in mortality rates between the United States and other countries found substantially higher colon cancer survival rates for American elderly seniors (those over age 75), in large part because screening did not decline with age in the United States.[32] While other countries limit access to screening and treatment for older individuals in ways that raise death rates, the United States' death rates decline relative to its peers as seniors age, precisely because American seniors maintain access to treatments.

Single-payer supporters often claim that the United States' poor life expectancy rate compared to other developed countries reflects a poor health system, making the argument for socialized medicine. However, many other factors also affect Americans' health relative to other countries—for instance, our much more heterogeneous population when compared to smaller European nations.

Moreover, Americans' higher obesity rates appear to affect death and life expectancy rates, as do higher rates of violent deaths (both homicides and suicides).[33] These issues may provide some commentary on American *society*, but they do not directly speak to the merits of America's *health-care system* relative to its peers'.

On that front, the United States has long boasted superior

---

32 Jessica Ho and Samuel Preston, "U.S. Mortality in an International Context: Age Variations," *Population and Development Review* 2010, https://www.ncbi.nlm.nih.gov/pmc/articles/PMC3140845/.

33 Ibid.

outcomes from cancer treatment—the leading cause of death in developed nations—than its European counterparts. For individuals diagnosed during the years 1995-1999, American patients had an average survival rate of 11.1 years, or nearly 16% greater than the 9.3 years faced by European patients.[34] The survival gap between American and European patients has remained constant going back for more than a decade.[35]

Moreover, while Americans spend more on cancer treatment than Europeans, they also receive more benefits, in the form of longer survival times. From 1983 through 1999, American patients received a net financial benefit—that is, increased survival compared to their European peers, even after accounting for higher spending levels—of $598 billion, or about $43 billion per year.[36]

Better access to treatment, better survival times, and more benefits to patients—the arguments for the American health system over single payer seem obvious, except to those on the left.

THE VA SCANDAL EPITOMIZES SINGLE PAYER'S PROBLEMS

Liberals must also face the flaws exposed in a single-payer system already operating in the United States: The Veterans Health Administration. The waiting times scandal within the VA, which exploded into public view in early 2014, hints at the future the United States could face under a nationwide

---

34 Tomas Philipson, *et al.*, "An Analysis of Whether Higher Health Care Spending in the United States versus Europe Is 'Worth It' in the Case of Cancer," *Health Affairs,* April 2012, https://www.healthaffairs.org/doi/full/10.1377/hlthaff.2011.1298.

35 Ibid.

36 Ibid.

single-payer system. Veterans who survived battles in far-flung places from Normandy to Vietnam to Iraq could not survive their encounters with a bureaucratic culture that denied patients timely access to care.

Some of the ingredients that precipitated the VA scandal closely resemble the problems seen in other single-payer systems worldwide. For one, under-funding and an aging patient population, a problem magnified in the VA's case by an explosion of veterans from conflicts in Iraq and Afghanistan while Vietnam and World War II vets grow older and more infirm. Then there's its bureaucratic culture focused on meeting targets, even if it involves cutting corners to do so, and decades full of warnings that veterans were incurring wait times far longer than those publicly advertised.[37]

Those factors all culminated in horrific stories like that of Thomas Breen, a 71-year-old Navy veteran. In late September 2013, Breen went to the emergency room at the Phoenix VA hospital with blood in his urine.

Despite his symptoms, his prior history of cancer, and notations on the chart marking his case as "urgent," Breen was sent home to wait—and wait—for an appointment with a urologist. Despite the urgency of his case, and his family's regular efforts to get an appointment, not even a VA primary care doctor would see Breen—until he died on November 30, 2013, of Stage IV bladder cancer.[38]

---

37   United States Government Accountability Office, "Veterans Health Care: VA Needs Better Data on Extent and Causes of Wait Times," Report GAO/HEHS-00-90, May 2000, https://www.gao.gov/assets/240/230347.pdf.

38   Scott Bronstein and Drew Griffin, "A Fatal Wait: Veterans Anguish and Die on a VA Hospital's Secret List," CNN, April 23, 2014, https://www.cnn.com/2014/04/23/health/veterans-dying-health-care-delays/.

Breen's children described his agonizing last days, in which he recognized that the VA system established to help veterans like him had let him down in ways that hastened his death:

> At the end is when he suffered. He screamed. He cried. And that's something I'd never seen him do before, was cry. Never. Never. He cried in the kitchen right here. "Don't let me die....Why is this happening to me? Why won't anybody help me?"[39]

On December 6, 2013, more than two months after Breen's initial ER visit, his children received a telephone call: The VA finally had an appointment available for their father—who had died a week earlier, thanks in no small part to the agency's neglect.[40]

Breen's case represented a symptom of a larger problem with single-payer systems. As a review ordered by President Obama concluded, the VA had developed a "corrosive culture" that affected morale, one in which VA staffers themselves called the organization's behavior "unethical" and injurious to patients.[41]

Scathing as the reviews of the scandal proved, few should find them surprising. When single-payer systems lack adequate funding—and most will lack funding sooner or later because they drive up health spending—the supply of care will not meet available demand, and waiting times will almost inevitably result.

Other government-run health plans also result in poor health

---

39   Ibid.

40   Ibid.

41   Jim Kuhnhenn, "VA Review Finds 'Significant and Chronic' Failures," NBC News, June 27, 2014, https://www.nbcnews.com/news/us-news/veterans-affairs-review-finds-significant-chronic-failures-n143151.

outcomes for patients. For instance, the Oregon Health Insurance Experiment revealed poor outcomes for patients on Medicaid.[42] The experiment tracked patients randomly selected to enroll in the Medicaid program, and compared their results with a similar set of lower-income patients who remained uninsured.

A series of papers compared the results of the Oregon residents newly enrolled in Medicaid, and they did not speak well of Medicaid's effects on patients' health. One paper showed no measurable improvement in patients' physical health outcomes when compared to individuals who remained uninsured.[43]

A second paper showed that patients' use of the emergency room increased by 40% after obtaining Medicaid coverage. That increase in ER usage persisted over several years, suggesting that poor reimbursement levels encourage Medicaid beneficiaries to use the emergency room, rather than a doctor, as a prime source of health care.[44]

Medicaid beneficiaries have complained about poor access to doctors for years, such that some of them do not consider Medicaid "real insurance."[45] In just a few years, all Americans could face such a situation, with no real options if a single-payer system in the United States, like single-payer systems in other countries, lets them down.

---

42   More information available at http://www.nber.org/oregon/.

43   Katherine Baicker, *et al.*, "The Oregon Experiment: Effects of Medicaid on Clinical Outcomes," *New England Journal of Medicine,* May 2, 2013, https://www.nejm.org/doi/full/10.1056/NEJMsa1212321.

44   Amy Finkelstein, *et al.*, "Effect of Medicaid Coverage on ED Use: Further Evidence from Oregon's Experiment," *New England Journal of Medicine,* October 20, 2016, http://www.nejm.org/doi/full/10.1056/NEJMp1609533.

45   Vanessa Fuhrmans, "Note to Medicaid Patients: The Doctor Won't See You," *Wall Street Journal,* July 19, 2007, https://www.wsj.com/articles/SB118480165648770935.

NO EXIT

One big difference separates these prior stories with the vision of single-payer health care the Left envisions in the United States. In the examples above, individuals dissatisfied with the government-run plan have options of their own. Thanks in part to the Chaoulli ruling, Canadian patients can purchase private insurance to cover the cost of their care. Indeed, private spending accounts for nearly 30% of all health expenditures in Canada.[46]

Likewise, patients in Britain can buy supplemental coverage to pay for treatments the NHS will not cover.[47] At home, new veterans' choice legislation, signed into law by President Trump in June 2018, will give them more private options should they face long waits within the VA system.[48]

But the House and Senate single-payer bills will make private health insurance "unlawful" in the United States, giving patients few if any options if the government-run health plan denies them access to care. Under the legislation, patients could continue pay for treatment entirely out of pocket, but only the richest individuals can afford to fund treatments like cancer drugs, or personalized gene therapies, that easily cost into the hundreds of thousands of dollars per year.

Single-payer supporters may claim that the ban on private health coverage represents an attempt, however ham-handed, to

---

46   Sara Allin and David Rudoler, "The Canadian Health Care System," in Elias Mossialos, *et al.*, eds., *International Profiles of Health Care Systems*, Commonwealth Fund, May 2017, https://www.commonwealthfund.org/sites/default/files/documents/___media_files_publications_fund_report_2017_may_mossialos_intl_profiles_v5.pdf, p. 21.

47   Quoted in Ruth Thorlby and Sandeepa Arora, "The English Health Care System," in Mossialos, *et al.*, eds., *International Profiles*, p. 49.

48   VA MISSION Act, P.L. 115-182.

promote "fairness" within the health system. After all, prohibiting private insurance attempts to prevent a two-speed healthcare system, in which wealthier individuals can buy their way to the front of the queue.

But even with that prohibition removed, a single-payer system would impose hardships on untold millions of American patients. Eliminating the ban on private insurance would allow *some* people to opt out of the government system—but certainly not all, or even most. As it is, even with private insurance prohibited, individuals with financial means would still have opportunities to use their financial resources to overcome government-imposed restrictions on access to costly treatments.

To put it simply, the rich will always find ways to obtain access to treatments—whether through private insurance, private care, or both. But the most vulnerable patients, and those of more modest means, will have to take whatever "options" the government-run health plan offers—and experience suggests those options will leave much to be desired.

If single-payer legislation passes, the federal government will have near-total control over your health care. History demonstrates that control will result in government not providing prompt coverage of some patients' costly treatments. And when government blocks the use of therapies on cost grounds, vulnerable patients will have little ability to access needed care.

This dystopian future awaits American patients under the House and Senate single-payer bills. But other legislative proposals pushed by the Left will also lead to the same bleak outcome of total government control—albeit slightly more slowly.

8

THE "CAMEL'S NOSE" APPROACH TO ENACTING SINGLE PAYER

KEY POINTS

- Even so-called "incremental" health-care proposals, like those creating a government-run "public option" for health insurance, will eventually lead to single payer—as supporters of such proposals admit.

- Because it can reimburse doctors and hospitals at rates much lower than private insurance, a government-run plan would attract millions of individuals away from private health coverage.

- In 2009, the non-partisan Lewin Group concluded that a government-run health plan, roughly equivalent to several current proposals, would cause 119.1 million individuals to drop or lose their private health coverage.

- Any government-run health plan would also have other structural advantages not available to private insurers—for instance, the ability to receive taxpayer funds from the Treasury.

- Liberals want to create a single-payer system, and they would sabotage private health coverage to boost a government-run health plan to achieve this goal, even if done more slowly than immediate single-payer.

On April 18, 2009, Rep. Jan Schakowsky (D-IL) spoke at a health-care rally in Chicago. A member of the House Energy and Commerce Committee, which has primary congressional jurisdiction over health care, Schakowsky told the crowd of liberal activists she supported their goal of a single-payer health-care system:

> I know that many of you here today are single payer advocates [loud cheering], and so am I. I'm a cosponsor of [H.R.] 676 [a single-payer bill]. And those of us who are pushing for a public health insurance option don't disagree with the goal. This is not a principled fight. This is a fight about strategy for getting there—and I believe we will.[1]

---

1   Rep. Jan Schakowsky, remarks at Health Care for America Rally, April 18, 2009, video available at https://www.youtube.com/watch?v=W_MtLyDfXJA.

She explained that creating a government-run health plan, or a "public option," would lead to single-payer advocates' ultimate goal, recounting events at the White House's health-care summit a few weeks previously:

> And next to me was a guy from the insurance company, who then argued against the public health insurance option, saying it wouldn't let private insurance compete—that a public option will put the private insurance industry out of business and lead to single payer. [Loud cheering.] My single-payer friends, he was right! The man was right![2]

Schakowsky's comments illustrate the problems with the supposed "incremental" strategies Democrats advocate to the general public. Lumped into a broad category of "Medicare for More," these proposals would try to expand the number of individuals on government coverage (whether Medicare, Medicaid, or both) while retaining some role for private insurance—at least in the short term.

But Schakowsky's comments show that, at their core, most liberal policy-makers don't believe in giving patients choice in health care, or in the power of competition to provide better-quality care. Schakowsky doesn't just think that a government-run health plan will lead to single payer. Her comments very clearly indicate that she wants to bring about such an outcome.

Liberals view the number of people with private insurance as a *political problem* to overcome. They want to get to single payer, but they recognize that throwing more than 180 million Americans off of employer-sponsored coverage presents an

---

2   Ibid.

obstacle to objective. These policy-makers don't actually believe in the private provision of health coverage, but will include some short-term nods in that direction, largely to appease public opinion.

Take for instance Jacob Hacker, the Yale University professor who helped popularize the concept of a government-run "public option" for health insurance.[3] At a July 2008 policy forum, Hacker explained that he, like Schakowsky, wants to end up with a single-payer system, and thinks a government-run plan will lead to such an outcome:

> Someone once said to me this is a Trojan horse for single payer. And I said, "Well, it's not a Trojan horse, right? It's just right there!" I'm telling you—we're going to get there. Over time, slowly, but we'll move away from reliance on employment-based health insurance—as we should—but we'll do it in a way that we're not going to frighten people into thinking they're going to lose their private insurance.[4]

Note the contradictory nature of Hacker's comments: He does not want to "frighten people into thinking they're going to lose their private insurance," even though he thinks "we're going to get" to a single-payer system—which involves people losing their private insurance.

The fact that advocates of a government-run health plan *want* these various "incremental" proposals to lead to single payer demonstrates precisely why they should concern American patients.

---

3   Jia Lynn Yang, "The Man Who Invented Health Care's 'Public Option,'" *Fortune,* September 4, 2009, http://archive.fortune.com/2009/09/04/news/economy/public_option_hacker.fortune/index.htm.

4   Video available at https://www.youtube.com/watch?v=3sTfZJBYo1I.

Despite claims that a government-run plan will compete on a "level playing field" with private coverage, Schakowsky, Hacker, and the like will design policies to put a thumb—more like a fist—firmly on the scale in favor of the government plan. Over time, and likely sooner rather than later, the government-run "option" will become the only "option" people have, putting the United States on the expressway to single-payer health care.

THE "INCREMENTAL" PROPOSALS, EXPLAINED

Democrats have introduced many pieces of legislation to revise or expand Obamacare's subsidy scheme, expand government-run health coverage, or some combination of the two.[5] Essentially, these bills would make health care more "affordable" by expanding government price controls, using Americans' hard-earned taxpayer dollars to subsidize coverage for some portion of the population, or both. Noteworthy proposals in these categories include the following:

Medicare Buy-In:

Sen. Debbie Stabenow (D-MI) introduced this legislation as S. 470, the Medicare at 50 Act.[6] Under the bill, individuals could buy into the Medicare program, including Medicare Advantage, once they turn 50. Enrollees would pay a monthly premium, equal to the full cost of providing Medicare benefits for the eligible population (i.e., people ages 50-64).

---

5   The summaries provided here include a discussion of the respective bills' major provisions, as they relate to the expansion of Medicare and Medicaid and the functioning of insurance Exchanges. These brief summaries are not intended to be comprehensive, as many of the bills contain other provisions.

6   Unless otherwise noted, all bill numbers refer to legislative proposals introduced in the 116th Congress, which began in January 2019 and continues through 2020.

While the federal government pays for 75% of Medicare beneficiaries' Part B premiums, enrollees in the buy-in program would not automatically receive a government subsidy. However, individuals who qualify for Obamacare insurance subsidies—those without an offer of "affordable" employer coverage, and with family incomes below 400% of the federal poverty level ($103,000 for a family of four in 2019)—could use those subsidies to defray their premiums for the Medicare buy-in program.

In the House, Rep. Brian Higgins (D-NY) has introduced similar legislation as H.R. 1346. In addition to the Medicare buy-in for individuals over 50, the Higgins bill also includes "stabilization" provisions for Obamacare exchanges. These "stability" provisions would reinstate federal programs of reinsurance—subsidizing insurers for some of the expenses high-cost patients incur—and risk corridors—reimbursing insurance plans with large losses, offset (in whole or in part) by payments to the federal government from plans with large profits—that under Obamacare expired in 2016.[7] The bill would also provide increased cost-sharing assistance (i.e., lower deductibles and co-payments) for households with incomes lower than 400% of the federal poverty level.

Government-Run "Public Option":
These proposals also allow individuals to buy into the Medicare program. However, unlike the Stabenow and Higgins

---

[7] For more information on Obamacare's original reinsurance and risk corridor programs, see Chris Jacobs, "Obamacare's $170.8 Billion in Insurer Bailouts," *National Review,* June 7, 2016, https://www.nationalreview.com/2016/06/obamacare-bailouts-billions-billions-billions-cant-keep-insurers-afloat/.

bills—which limit the buy-in to individuals over 50—these bills permit individuals of any age to purchase Medicare coverage. These proposals more closely resemble the government-run "public option" that Democrats proposed, but rejected, while debating Obamacare in 2009-10.

Sen. Tim Kaine (D-VA) and declared 2020 presidential candidate Sen. Michael Bennet (D-CO) have introduced one version of this proposal, S. 981, the Medicare-X Choice Act. The bill would make a government-run health plan available to individuals on the Obamacare exchanges. The plan would phase in over several years, beginning in 2021 in areas with no choice of insurer on their exchanges. By 2024, the plan would extend to the nationwide individual health insurance market, and in 2025 would extend to small business coverage.

Under the Medicare-X Choice Act, the government-run plan would reimburse doctors and hospitals at Medicare rates; however, the secretary of Health and Human Services (HHS) could increase those rates "by up to 25 percent" for items and services furnished in rural areas. Medical providers would be required to participate in the plan in order to participate in Medicare and Medicaid. The legislation would also reinstate a reinsurance mechanism for the Obamacare exchanges, and increase the Obamacare subsidy regime, removing the income cap on eligibility (currently set at 400% of the poverty level, or $103,000 for a family of four in 2019) and capping premiums at 13% of household income for affluent households (low-income families would pay a smaller percentage of income).

Sens. Sheldon Whitehouse (D-RI) and Sherrod Brown (D-OH) have introduced their own version of this proposal as S. 1033, the CHOICE Act; Rep. Jan Schakowsky (D-IL) introduced a House companion as H.R. 2085. The legislation would establish a government-run health plan on the exchanges, beginning in 2020. The HHS secretary would set premiums for the plan, and "negotiate" with providers regarding their reimbursement levels; however, if the secretary and providers do not agree, reimbursement rates would default to Medicare levels. All doctors and hospitals currently participating in Medicare or Medicaid would be deemed participating in the government-run plan, unless such providers affirmatively opt out.

Sen. Ben Cardin (D-MD) has introduced another version of this proposal, the Keeping Health Insurance Affordable Act, S.3. His legislation would also establish a government-run health plan, available only through the exchanges. The government-run plan would reimburse doctors at Medicare rates for its first three years (2020 through 2022). For 2023 and future years, the HHS secretary would also set rates administratively (i.e., through government fiat), but the new rates could not "increase average medical costs per enrollee" compared to continuing under the Medicare reimbursement formulae.

Doctors currently participating in Medicare would automatically be considered participating in the government-run plan, but could opt out "in a process established by the Secretary." The legislation would also increase eligibility for Obamacare premium subsidies to households with incomes lower than 600% of poverty ($154,500 for a family of four in 2019; the current limit is $103,000, or 400% of poverty), and includes several provisions related to prescription drug pricing.

Finally, Sen. Jeff Merkley (D-OR) has introduced his own Medicare plan, which he calls Medicare Part E. Under his Choose Medicare Act (S. 1261), the Medicare Part E plan would offer all of Obamacare's required benefits, including abortion coverage. Any individual could enroll in the plan, except those already eligible for the current Medicare and Medicaid programs. The Centers for Medicare and Medicaid Services would develop a plan to enroll interested employers in the program.

Under the Merkley Medicare Part E plan, the new program would "negotiate" rates with doctors and hospitals. Payments could not total less than the current Medicare program, but could not exceed the average rates paid by insurers on the Obamacare exchanges. The plan would deem providers participating in the current Medicare program participants in the new Medicare Part E, and would prohibit participating providers from balance billing their patients. (To use a hypothetical example, balance billing might occur when a doctor charges $100 for a service, and patient's insurer reimburses only $50. Under balance billing, a doctor would attempt to charge the patient the $50 difference in reimbursement, plus any co-payment insurance might require.)

The Merkley legislation would appropriate $2 billion to establish Medicare Part E, along with additional funds for program reserves. It includes additional provisions related to the current Medicare program—imposing an out-of-pocket limit on beneficiary cost-sharing, and requiring "negotiation" of prescription drug prices.

In addition, Merkley bill would increase funding for Obamacare in several respects. It would authorize funding for the law's navigator programs, and appropriate $10 billion per year from 2020 through 2022 ($30 billion total) to fund reinsurance programs in every state. The bill would expand eligibility for Obamacare's insurance subsidies up to 600% of poverty ($154,500 for a family of four in 2019). The legislation would also link those subsidies to more generous insurance coverage—gold plans, with an actuarial value (the percentage of an average enrollee's health expenses paid by insurance) of 80%, rather than silver plans, with an actuarial value of 70%. And the bill would further reduce cost-sharing for low-income beneficiaries.

Medicaid Buy-In:

Sen. Brian Schatz (D-HI) has introduced S. 489, which would give states the option to allow individuals to buy into the Medicaid program. For individuals participating in the buy-in program, states could impose "premiums, deductibles, cost-sharing, or other similar charges that are actuarially fair." However, states could not charge anyone a premium greater than 9.5% of household income, and must abide by Obamacare's rating restrictions (i.e., vary premiums only by age, family size, geography, and tobacco use).

The Schatz bill also includes provisions designed to encourage recalcitrant states to expand Medicaid to the able-bodied, by providing a 100% federal match for the first three years states take up the expansion. (Under current law, the 100% match for expansion populations applied to calendar years 2014-16 only.) In the House, Rep. Ben Ray Lujan (D-NM) has introduced similar legislation to the Schatz bill as H.R. 1277.

Healthy America:

This proposal does not exist as a piece of legislation—at least not yet. Rather, a group of researchers at the liberal Urban Institute fashioned this proposal in 2018, to outline a potential way forward for Democrats on health care.[8] Effectively, the plan would

---

8   Linda Blumberg, John Holahan, and Stephen Zuckerman, "The Healthy America Plan: Building on the Best of Medicare and the Affordable Care Act," Urban Institute, May 11, 2018, https://www.urban.org/sites/default/files/publication/98432/2001826_2018.05.11_healthy_america_final_1.pdf.

retain a role for employer coverage and the current Medicare program, but consolidate most other forms of insurance into a new program.

The plan proposes combining most current Medicaid enrollees and participants on the Obamacare exchanges into a new "super-exchange," called Healthy America. Individuals could purchase private or publicly offered insurance plans—as in the current Medicare program—but insurance offered through Healthy America would pay doctors and hospitals at Medicare rates, "with some adjustments" possible "to encourage plan availability in all markets."[9]

The plan would also increase subsidies for policies offered through Healthy America compared to the current Obamacare subsidies. No household would pay more than 8.5% of its income in premiums, regardless of its income, as opposed to Obamacare, which offers subsidies only to households with incomes less than 400% of poverty ($103,000 for a family of four in 2019).

The plan would retain the current system of employer-sponsored coverage; however, individuals could decline their employer plan and still receive subsidies for Healthy America coverage. (Obamacare contains a "firewall," such that individuals with an offer of "affordable" employer coverage cannot qualify for exchange subsidies.[10]) The plan would also reinstitute an individual mandate to purchase health coverage, with an accompanying tax penalty.[11]

---

9   Ibid., p. 7.

10   Section 1401(a) of the Patient Protection and Affordable Care Act, P.L. 111-148, codified at 26 U.S.C. 36B(c)(2)(B).

11   Chris Jacobs, "Democrats Consider How to Reinstate the Individual Mandate under a Different Name," *Federalist,* May 17, 2018, https://thefederalist.com/2018/05/17/democrats-consider-reinstate-individual-mandate-different-name/.

Medicare for America:

Introduced by Rep. Rosa DeLauro (D-CT) as H.R. 2452, this plan has its roots in a proposal offered by the liberal Center for American Progress.[12] The bill would create a temporary government-run health plan for the years 2021 and 2022. That plan would pay medical providers Medicare reimbursement rates, and automatically declare any provider participating in Medicare or Medicaid as of the date of enactment a participating provider for the new government-run health plan. The plan would cover the full complement of Obamacare-mandated benefits, including abortion coverage. It would also prohibit providers from failing to perform abortions or other covered services "because of their religious objections."[13]

Beginning in 2023, the bill would create the Medicare for America program. The program would automatically enroll individuals at birth, when they become eligible for Medicare (i.e., turn 65), or who lack "qualified health coverage." By 2025, the bill would incorporate existing Medicare populations into the program, and by 2027, the bill would incorporate existing Medicaid populations into the program. After that time, the only options for "qualified health coverage" outside the program would include qualified employer coverage (including Tricare and the Federal Employees Health Benefit Program), coverage through the

---

12   Center for American Progress, "Medicare Extra for All: A Plan to Guarantee Universal Health Coverage in the United States," February 2018, https://cdn. americanprogress.org/content/uploads/2018/02/21130514/MedicareExtra-report.pdf; Chris Jacobs, "Liberals Have a New Plan to Take Over the Health Care System—What You Need to Know," *Federalist* February 23, 2018, https:// thefederalist.com/2018/02/23/center-for-american-progress-drops-new-government-run-health-plan/.

13   Section 105(b)(3) of H.R. 2452, the Medicare for America Act of 2019.

Department of Veterans Affairs, and the Indian Health Service.

The bill specifically makes the provision of private health insurance "unlawful," except for qualified employer coverage. However, unlike the single-payer bills, private insurers could offer Medicare Advantage for America plans as part of the new program (similar to Medicare Advantage today).

The bill prescribes premiums and maximum cost-sharing amounts. Households with incomes less than 200% of poverty ($51,500 for a family of four in 2019) would pay no premiums, while those with incomes greater than 600% of poverty ($154,500 for a family of four in 2019) would pay 8% of their income in premiums. Likewise, households with incomes less than 200% of poverty will pay no cost-sharing at all; those with incomes greater than 600% of poverty will pay no more than $5,000 in total out-of-pocket expenses per family. The bill eliminates all deductibles for Medicare for America plans.

In addition to prohibiting providers from balance billing patients, the bill prohibits any provider "from entering into a private contract with an individual enrolled under Medicare for America for any item or service coverable under Medicare for America."[14] The legislation would automatically enroll Americans in the new program, and would only permit individuals to opt out who have "qualified health coverage" from certain employers.[15] Therefore, the ban on private contracting would effectively prohibit most Americans from opting out of the government system. To put it bluntly, this provision would prevent most Americans

---

14   Proposed Section 2205(f) of the Social Security Act, as included in Section 111 of H.R. 2452.

15   Proposed Section 2202(b)(4) of the Social Security Act, as included in Section 111 of H.R. 2452.

from obtaining private health care—*even with their own money*.[16]

The program would pay doctors and medical providers Medicare or Medicaid rates, whichever is greater, and would pay hospitals 110% of those current Medicare or Medicaid payment levels. All participating providers in Medicare would be deemed providers for the new program. The secretary could also increase rates "to ensure adequate access to care."

Large employers—those with more than 100 employees—would face a "pay or play" mandate. They could continue to maintain their employer plans, provided their plan covers at least 80% of an average employee's health expenses and the employer pays at least 70% of premiums. If they do not, they must make a contribution equal to 8% of annual payroll to fund the new program.

Small employers with fewer than 100 employees could continue to maintain their current coverage, but would not face a penalty if they do not. Workers could decline an offer of employer coverage to enroll in the new program without penalty, in which case the employer (regardless of the firm's size) must make a contribution for the worker's coverage equal to the firm's contribution for the worker's employer-provided coverage.

This bill, unlike the single-payer bills and other pieces of legislation described above, includes explicit tax increases to pay for the new program. Those tax provisions include:

---

16   Chris Jacobs, "This New Democratic Plan Would Ban Private Medicine," *Wall Street Journal,* May 13, 2019, https://www.wsj.com/articles/dems-new-plan-would-ban-private-medicine-11557688457.

- The full repeal of the 2017 Tax Cuts and Jobs Act;

- A 5% surtax on the adjusted gross income of every taxpayer in excess of $500,000 (a threshold *not* increased for inflation);

- Repeal of the "stepped-up" basis for calculating taxes on inherited gains;[17]

- A 3.1% increase in payroll taxes paid by individuals—on top of the 8% payroll tax assessed on large employers not providing coverage, as explained above;

- Termination of Health Savings Accounts and Flexible Spending Arrangements;

- Increases in tobacco and alcohol taxes;

- A new tax on sugar-sweetened beverages, equal to one penny for every 4.2 grams of "caloric sweetener" included in such products; and

- A repeal of Obamacare's excise tax on high-cost health plans—a provision that Congress has repeatedly delayed, but which under current law will take effect beginning in 2022.

---

17   For instance, when Mr. X dies, a stock he initially paid $5 to buy is worth $20. Ms. Y inherits the stock from Mr. X, and sells it at $30 per share. Under current tax law, Ms. Y would pay taxes on a realized gain of $10 per share—$30 minus $20—the "stepped-up basis" under which she inherited the stock. Under the proposal, Ms. Y would pay taxes on a realized gain of $25 per share—$30 minus Mr. X's original purchase price of $5.

The bill also includes a series of other provisions, including elimination of the 24-month waiting period for individuals with disabilities to qualify for Medicare benefits, an expansion of coverage for long-term services and supports, mandatory nurse staffing requirements for hospitals, and provisions related to prescription drug pricing.

TAKING A RIDE ON THE SLIPPERY SLOPE

Each of these pieces of legislation would accelerate the march to single payer, on multiple levels. First, and most obviously, they all attempt to "piggyback" on existing reimbursement rates paid by government programs, which pay doctors and hospitals far less than private insurers do.

As we have seen, Medicare currently pays doctors 75% of private insurance rates, and hospitals 60% of private insurance.[18] Likewise, Medicaid pays doctors about 54% of private insurance rates, and hospitals about 61%.[19] And Medicare and Medicaid payment rates are expected to decline further when compared to private insurance in the coming years, due to scheduled reductions in reimbursement formulae.[20]

As Medicare and Medicaid reimbursement rates decline, enrollment has increased in these programs—due to the

---

18   John Shatto and Kent Clemens, "Projected Medicare Expenditures under an Illustrative Scenario with Alternative Payment Updates to Medicare Providers," Centers for Medicare and Medicaid Services Office of the Actuary memorandum, April 22, 2019, https://www.cms.gov/Research-Statistics-Data-and-Systems/Statistics-Trends-and-Reports/ReportsTrustFunds/Downloads/2019TRAlternativeScenario.pdf.

19   Ibid.

20   Ibid.

retirement of the Baby Boomers and the expansion of Medicaid under Obamacare, respectively. As more and more people enroll in programs that pay providers less and less, two linked trends have occurred:

- Hospitals have significantly increased their posted charges as a percentage of Medicare rates, with average charges rising from 181% of Medicare rates in 2006 to 256% of Medicare rates in 2016; and

- The private-payer ratio of charges to costs "has increased to its historically highest level," rising from 1.30 in 2006 to 1.52 in 2016.[21]

Put more simply, hospitals are charging patients with private insurance more because government programs are paying them less. With hospitals losing sizable sums on Medicare patients— the average hospital had a -9.9% profit margin on Medicare patients in 2017, a loss projected to increase to 11% in 2019— patients with private insurance help to pick up the proverbial slack.[22] But what happens when there are fewer people with private insurance to do so?

---

21   Medicare Payment Advisory Commission, *A Data Book: Health Care Spending and the Medicare Program*, June 15, 2018, http://medpac.gov/docs/default-source/data-book/jun18_databookentirereport_sec.pdf?sfvrsn=0, pp. 84-85.

22   Medicare Payment Advisory Commission, *Report to the Congress: Medicare Payment Policy*, March 15, 2019, http://medpac.gov/docs/default-source/reports/mar19_medpac_entirereport_sec.pdf?sfvrsn=0, p. 89.

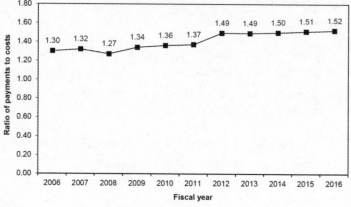

Chart 6-26. **Change in the private-payer ratio of payments to costs for hospital services, 2006–2016**

Medicare Payment Advisory Commission, June 2018.

Because the government-run plan would use Medicare or Medicaid reimbursement rates that are substantially lower than private health insurance payments, private insurers will have little ability to compete based on price. The government-run plan will offer lower premiums, because it will force hospitals and doctors to accept less pay for their services, siphoning off millions of patients.

In response, medical providers, particularly ones with large market share in uncompetitive markets, may try to raise charges on their privately insured customers, to compensate for the greater losses incurred by patients moving to the government-run health plan. But if they charge patients with private insurance more, that will lead to higher premiums—and more people switching to the government-run health plan. Medical providers would face a no-win situation, and private insurance could easily face a "death spiral," whereby a cycle of premium increases sends more and more people into the government-run health plan, making it a de facto single-payer system.

During the Obamacare debate in 2009, non-partisan actuaries at the Lewin Group predicted this very phenomenon. Their analysis concluded that a government-run health plan reimbursing providers at Medicare rates would have premiums 26% lower than private coverage for an individual, and 22% lower for a family.[23] If such a government-run health plan were open to all individuals, Lewin concluded that 119.1 million Americans—more than half of those with employer-based health coverage—would drop their private insurance to enroll in the government plan.[24]

As Schakowsky so famously claimed in her April 2009 remarks, this government-run health plan would very quickly lead to single payer. Even if some employers wanted to try and keep their existing health plans, the rapid erosion of private insurance would quickly lead all but the most stubborn or foolhardy from maintaining their coverage offerings. Moreover, Democrats would likely use other political means to weaken, and ultimately eliminate, private health insurance.

A RIGGED SYSTEM IN FAVOR OF GOVERNMENT-RUN CARE

To see how the Left would work to neuter private health

---

23   John Sheils and Randy Haught, "The Cost and Coverage Impacts of a Public Plan: Alternative Design Options," Lewin Group Staff Working Paper #4, April 8, 2009, https://web.archive.org/web/20100611011954/http://www.lewin.com/content/publications/LewinCostandCoverageImpactsofPublicPlan-Alternative%20DesignOptions.pdf, p. 4.

24   Ibid., Figure 3, Public Plan Enrollment and Reduction in Private Coverage Under a Public Plan Using Medicare Payment Levels, p. 5.

insurance when compared to government programs, look at how private Medicare Advantage plans "compete" with traditional Medicare. When seniors sign up for Medicare, they're not automatically enrolled in the lowest-cost plan. Seniors aren't enrolled in the plan with the closest doctors, or the best care for their specific health conditions. No, seniors are automatically enrolled in the *government-run* plan.

Making the government-run plan the default for seniors gives traditional Medicare a major advantage against Medicare Advantage plans. Medicare Advantage plans must engage in intensive marketing efforts, and offer better benefits, to lure patients away from traditional Medicare. Yet the same experts who claim to want "financial neutrality" between the government-run plan and Medicare Advantage never acknowledge, let alone attempt to quantify, the financial advantage traditional Medicare receives as the default enrollment option.[25]

Even as Democrats claimed during the Obamacare debate that they would create a government-run "public option" on a "level playing field" with private insurance, Obamacare did the exact opposite with Medicare Advantage. As part of his budget proposal to Congress, President Obama outlined what he called

---

25 See for instance Medicare Payment Advisory Commission, *Report to the Congress: Medicare Payment Policy*, March 15, 2009, http://medpac.gov/docs/default-source/reports/march-2009-report-to-congress-medicare-payment-policy.pdf?sfvrsn=0, Chapter 3, "The Medicare Advantage Program," pp. 251-69. Such claims of "financial neutrality" also ignore evidence that Medicare Advantage plans create "spillover" savings to traditional Medicare; see for instance Katherine Baicker, Michael Chernew, and Jacob Robbins, "The Spillover Effects of Medicare Managed Care: Medicare Advantage and Hospital Utilization," National Bureau of Economic Research Working Paper 19070, May 2013, http://www.nber.org/papers/w19070.pdf.

a "competitive bidding" program for Medicare Advantage.[26]

But did Obama and Democrats allow Medicare Advantage to compete against government-run Medicare, by making Medicare Advantage the default option if plans could provide benefits more cheaply than traditional Medicare? Absolutely not. They wouldn't dream of such a thing.

The bills described above include numerous provisions designed to "rig" the system in favor of the government-run option. To list but a few examples:

- Several of the bills automatically enroll doctors and hospitals in the government-run plan—meaning the plan, unlike private insurers, would not face the obstacle of forming a provider network. The Bennet-Kaine Medicare-X proposal requires providers to participate in the government-run plan as a condition of participation in Medicare and Medicaid—leverage that private insurers do not have.[27] The DeLauro Medicare for America bill goes even further: It says that doctors participating in the current Medicare program on the date of the bill's enactment "shall remain" providers in the new program, and includes no provision allowing current providers to opt out—ever.[28]

---

26   United States Office of Management and Budget, *A New Era of Responsibility: Renewing America's Promise*, Fiscal Year 2010 budget submission to Congress, February 26, 2009, https://www.govinfo.gov/content/pkg/BUDGET-2010-BUD/pdf/BUDGET-2010-BUD.pdf, p. 28.

27   Proposed Section 2208 of the Social Security Act, as included in Section 2 of S. 981, the Medicare-X Choice Act of 2019.

28   Proposed Section 2206(c) of the Social Security Act, as included in Section 111 of H.R. 2452.

- Several of the bills use Treasury dollars to provide seed funding, or money for reserves or administrative overhead, to the government-run plan. Private insurers have no automatic sources of funds to tap, and must raise dollars on the private market—if they can find parties willing to assume that risk. The Bennet-Kaine Medicare-X bill gives the government-run plan $1 billion in reserve funds, with no requirement for repayment.[29] The Merkley bill goes even further, giving its Medicare Part E $2 billion in start-up funding, plus additional reserve funds.[30] Both for these programs and others like them, Congress could also come back and grant a government-run plan additional taxpayer dollars, bailing out the program in a way that advantages the government plan compared to private insurers.

- By automatically enrolling individuals in government-run health coverage at birth, the DeLauro legislation would essentially convert the United States to a single-payer health program within a generation.[31] The Center for American Progress, which created the blueprint for this bill, admits that the auto-enrollment provision "ensures that [the government-run plan] would continue to increase in enrollment over time."[32]

---

29 Proposed Section 2201(b)(1) of the Social Security Act, as included in Section 2 of S. 981.

30 Proposed Section 2201(h) of the Social Security Act, as included in Section 2 of S.1261, the Choose Medicare Act.

31 Proposed Section 2202(b)(2)(A) of the Social Security Act, as included in Section 111 of H.R. 2452.

32 Center for American Progress, "Medicare Extra for All," p. 4.

All these provisions would give a government-run health plan major advantages over private insurance. Moreover, the mere establishment of a government-run health plan with these inherent advantages would send a clear signal to financial markets, scaring away potential investors in ways that could lower insurers' stock prices and choke off their access to capital.

Liberals have spent most of the time since President Trump's inauguration complaining about how he and his administration are "sabotaging" Obamacare by deliberately allowing the law to fail.[33] Ironically enough, however, that term aptly describes what liberals want to do to private health coverage, as the provisions above demonstrate. If ever a government-run plan competed against private insurance, the Left would find every conceivable way possible to sabotage the latter against the former, all to achieve their socialist dream of single-payer health care.

NEXT STOP: EXPRESSWAY TO SINGLE PAYER

Democrats' actions regarding private and government coverage render their words about a "level playing field" meaningless. For instance, Sen. Kirsten Gillibrand (D-NY)—a presidential candidate and a co-sponsor of Sanders's single-payer bill—said she "dared" private insurers to compete against a government-run health plan.[34] In an MSNBC town hall, she said she also supported a government-run "public option *as a transition*....

---

33   Chris Jacobs, "Let's Examine New Charges That Trump IS 'Sabotaging' Obamacare," *Federalist,* August 24, 2018, https://thefederalist.com/2018/08/24/lets-examine-new-charges-that-trump-is-sabotaging-obamacare/.

34   Elena Schneider, "Gillibrand Defends Handling of Harassment Complaints," *Politico,* March 18, 2019, https://www.politico.com/story/2019/03/18/kirsten-gillibrand-sexual-harassment-1226466.

I imagine within a few years, most Americans are going to choose Medicare because it's quality and more affordable."[35] [Emphasis added.]

As with Schakowsky and Hacker, Gillibrand's comments very clearly indicate that she *wants* to create a single-payer system, but would consider using a more politically palatable mechanism to arrive at that goal. Her comments also illustrate how her prediction that "most Americans are going to choose Medicare" will become a self-fulfilling prophecy, as she and her fellow Democrats will tilt the playing field so heavily in favor of a government-run health plan that it can become the "transition" to single payer they envision.

The evidence from their own words and proposals suggest that the Left wants to impose a single-payer health-care system on the United States—whether slowly or in one fell swoop, and whether the American people want it or not. To stave off the damaging consequences of such a change, conservatives need to articulate a better approach to fixing our health care markets.

---

35   Ibid.

9

A BETTER PATH FORWARD

KEY POINTS

- To fend off demands for single-payer health care, conservatives need to articulate a better alternative to it and the current system.

- Obamacare's pre-existing provisions served as the prime driver of a more-than-doubling in individual health insurance premiums, and have priced millions of individuals out of the market for coverage.

- Whereas liberals want to provide health coverage for people *after* they develop a pre-existing condition, conservatives should work to ensure people have quality, affordable coverage *before* they develop a costly disease.

- Rather than Obamacare's one-size-fits-all approach to pre-existing conditions, conservatives should promote a series of personalized alternatives.

- Promoting portable, individual insurance would put patients in charge of health care instead of employers or government bureaucrats.

- Making our safety net sustainable requires Congress to reform Medicaid and Medicare to make our current safety net sustainable.

- Properly aligning incentives within the health-care system would help slow the growth in health costs that threatens the nation's economic future.

As the old saying goes, you can't beat something with nothing. If conservatives want to stave off a full government takeover of health care, they need to articulate practical, better solutions that the American people can understand and accept.

Unfortunately, 2017 and 2018 saw Republicans in Congress fritter away a prime opportunity to articulate this type of vision. Predictably, the slogan "repeal-and-replace"—invented by staff for then-Senate Minority Leader Mitch McConnell (R-KY) at the time of Obamacare's passage—turned into "repeal-vs.-replace."[1] Conservative Republicans focused on repealing the law "root-and-branch," as McConnell himself famously

---

1   Carl Hulse, "'Repeal and Replace:' Words Still Hanging over G.O.P.'s Health Care Strategy," *New York Times,* January 15, 2017, https://www.nytimes.com/2017/01/15/us/politics/affordable-care-act-republicans-health-care.html; Chris Jacobs, "'Repeal and Replace' Becomes 'Repeal versus Replace,'" *National Review,* February 23, 2017, https://www.nationalreview.com/2017/02/repeal-obamacare-replace-obamacare-republicans-disagree/.

proclaimed in a 2013 speech, while moderates wanted to replace Obamacare with something that retained most, if not all, of its supposed benefits.[2]

The debate very quickly bogged down to where congressional Republicans fought over how much of Obamacare to keep. They ended up in a political "no-man's-land," with the worst of both worlds: Keeping enough of Obamacare to ensure premiums would remain high, and require massive subsidies to make coverage "affordable," while repealing enough of the law to allow Democrats to claim that they had "gutted" its preexisting condition provisions.[3]

Conservatives can only reframe the debate on health care by seizing it. As Margaret Thatcher famously observed, "First you win the argument—then you win the vote." But one can only win the argument—and the vote—by making it.

Unfortunately, many conservative lawmakers tend not to prioritize health care as an issue: They don't understand it, don't feel comfortable discussing the nuances of health policy, and only take a strong stand by outlining what they *oppose*—whether Obamacare, "Hillarycare," or single payer—rather than what they *support*.

But health-care entitlements represent a large, and growing, share of both federal and state budgets. That growth impedes the nation's ability to keep taxes low and maintain a strong

---

2   Jillian Rayfield, "Mitch McConnell at CPAC: Repeal Obamacare 'Root and Branch,'" *Salon,* March 15, 2013, https://www.salon.com/2013/03/15/mcconnell_at_cpac_repeal_obamacare_root_and_branch/.

3   Chris Jacobs, "How Republicans Shot Themselves in the Feet on Pre-Existing Conditions," *Federalist,* November 12, 2018, https://thefederalist.com/2018/11/12/republicans-shot-feet-pre-existing-conditions/.

national defense. On the state level, rising health-care spending means that Medicaid has tripled in size over the past three decades—growing from 9.7% of the average state budget in 1985 to 29.7% in 2018—crowding out other priorities like education, transportation, and law enforcement.[4]

Conservatives who care about any of these issues—from national security to transportation to state and federal taxes—*must* take an interest in health policy. Not only do their policy preferences depend on it—ordinary voters frustrated by the ever-rising cost of care will demand it. The principles outlined below provide a way forward for conservatives interested in outlining better solutions, ones that put the power to make health decisions back in the hands of doctors and patients, rather than bureaucrats.

ADDRESSING PRE-EXISTING CONDITIONS

After the 2018 campaign, discussion of almost any conservative health-care plan immediately comes back to one issue: What will you do about pre-existing conditions? To say that Republicans botched this issue in the midterm elections would put it mildly. Some failed to grasp the underlying policy, while many thought that repeating their support for pre-existing conditions would neutralize the issue.

---

4   National Association of State Budget Officers, "The State Expenditure Report," July 1987, https://higherlogicdownload.s3.amazonaws.com/NASBO/9d2d2db1-c943-4f1b-b750-0fca152d64c2/UploadedImages/SER%20Archive/ER_1987.PDF, "Medicaid Expenditures as a Percentage of Total Expenditures," p. 30; National Association of State Budget Officers, "2018 State Expenditure Report," November 2018, https://higherlogicdownload.s3.amazonaws.com/NASBO/9d2d2db1-c943-4f1b-b750-0fca152d64c2/UploadedImages/SER%20Archive/2018_State_Expenditure_Report_S.pdf, Table 29, Medicaid Expenditures as a Percentage of Total Expenditures, p. 56.

But the legislative proposals Congress considered in 2017 and 2018 helped put Republican lawmakers in a box of their own creation.[5] Those bills by and large retained two of Obamacare's pre-existing condition provisions—guaranteed issue, which requires insurers to accept all applicants regardless of health status, and community rating, which requires insurers to charge everyone the same premiums except for a few limited factors (age, family size, geography, and tobacco use). But the bills would have repealed, or allowed states to waive, two other provisions—essential health benefits, which tell insurers what types of treatments to include in their plans, and actuarial value, which tells insurers how much of the average person's health expenses their policies must cover.

Unfortunately, Republicans failed to understand two key points: one rooted in policy, the other in politics. First, the guaranteed issue and community rating provisions, and not the essential health benefits and actuarial value requirements, represented the "largest share of premium increases due to Obamacare."[6]

That conclusion comes from a March 2018 Heritage Foundation study. It analyzed the reasons premiums more than doubled for individual health insurance from 2013 (the year before Obamacare's major provisions took effect) to 2017.[7] Repealing, or allowing states to waive, other regulations, like

---

5   Jacobs, "How Republicans Shot Themselves in the Feet."

6   Edmund Haislmaier and Doug Badger, "How Obamacare Raised Premiums," Heritage Foundation *Backgrounder No. 3291*, March 5, 2018, https://www.heritage.org/sites/default/files/2018-03/BG3291.pdf.

7   Department of Health and Human Services Office of Planning and Evaluation, "ASPE Data Point: Individual Market Premium Changes: 2013-2017," May 23, 2017, https://aspe.hhs.gov/system/files/pdf/256751/IndividualMarketPremiumChanges.pdf.

essential health benefits and actuarial value, without also repealing the guaranteed issue and community rating requirements would bring only minor premium relief to insurance markets.[8]

Second, on pre-existing conditions, Democrats have no interest in splitting hairs over policy nuances. Particularly after their 2018 midterm election victories, which they attribute in large part to health care, they will attack *any* change to Obamacare's regulatory regime as "gutting" the pre-existing condition provisions. In May 2019, as Republicans noted, Democrats brought to the House floor legislation, entitled the Protecting Americans with Pre-Existing Conditions Act, that had at best a tangential relationship to pre-existing conditions.[9]

Liberals engaged in similar political gamesmanship over pre-existing conditions during the 2018 campaign, attacking Republican proposals to repeal or waive the essential health benefits and actuarial value provisions. As the *Washington Post* noted, Democrats even attacked one lawmaker, Rep. Brian Fitzpatrick (R-PA), who opposed "repeal-and-replace" legislation because he thought it undermined individuals with pre-existing conditions:

---

8   Chris Jacobs, "Americans Do Have 'Binary Choices' About Replacing Obamacare, But Not the Ones Paul Ryan Says," *Federalist,* April 4, 2017, https://thefederalist.com/2017/04/04/americans-binary-choices-replacing-obamacare-not-ones-paul-ryan-says/.

9   Juliegrace Brufke, "Republicans Troll Democrats with Proposals to Rename Upcoming Health Care Bill," *The Hill,* May 6, 2019, https://thehill.com/homenews/house/442418-republicans-troll-democrats-with-proposals-to-rename-upcoming-health-care-bill; H.R. 986, Protecting Americans with Pre-Existing Conditions Act of 2019.

The [Democratic Congressional Campaign Committee] really crosses the line here. Fitzpatrick bucked his party to vote against one of the President's top priorities, the repeal of Obamacare, specifically because he was concerned about the impact on people with pre-existing conditions. His reward? Being attacked for selling his constituents out on the issue because of his minor procedural votes....You would think Democrats would at least applaud him for his courage, but apparently that's not how the game is played these days.[10]

Accepting the leftist position didn't spare Fitzpatrick from Democratic attacks in 2018—and abject surrender won't spare other Republicans from similar attacks on pre-existing conditions either.

As with prior messaging campaigns from the Left, such as the "Mediscare" ads charging that House Budget Committee Chairman Paul Ryan (R-WI) wanted to throw seniors off a cliff, or the "War on Women" attacks about contraception coverage, when Democrats think they have a winning political issue, they won't give an inch.

To parry those attacks, conservatives should not expect that claiming support for Obamacare's pre-existing condition provisions will let them off the proverbial hook. Instead, recognizing that they will get attacked regardless, they should put forward their own better vision, consistent with common sense and human experience.

---

10   Glenn Kessler, "Democratic Attack Ad Falsely Knocks Republican on Pre-Existing Conditions," *Washington Post Fact Checker* blog, October 15, 2018, https://www. washingtonpost.com/politics/2018/10/15/democratic-attack-ad-falsely-knocks-republican-preexisting-conditions/?utm_term=.2ea54de07ccc.

BETTER SOLUTIONS FOR OBAMACARE'S FORGOTTEN VICTIMS
Conservative messaging on pre-existing conditions went off track when it neglected Obamacare's biggest victims.[11] Who can forget the 4.7 million individuals who received cancellation notices in fall 2013?[12] Many lost the health insurance they had and liked, leaving them without coverage when they developed pre-existing conditions.

I know one such individual, the father of a friend and former colleague. He and his wife lost their coverage in the fall of 2013, and when he was diagnosed with colon cancer, the consequences proved devastating:

> We turned to a Christian [health care] sharing ministry after Obamacare canceled our Blue Cross Blue Shield plan because it was the only affordable option we had. And we prayed we'd make it to 65 without getting sick. Unfortunately, that didn't happen. When we realized that I needed to get treatment at M.D. Anderson [Cancer Center] because of the tricky location of the tumor, the cost of entry was prohibitive because our sharing ministry plan was considered "self-pay" by the hospital. That's when my son started up a GoFundMe to get me in the door to get the care I needed.[13]
>
> God worked a miracle in that operating room. I'm cancer-free and back to a normal life. But the stress of the

---

11   Chris Jacobs, "What the Press Isn't Telling You About the Politics of Pre-Existing Conditions," *Federalist,* November 5, 2018, https://thefederalist.com/2018/11/05/press-isnt-telling-politics-pre-existing-conditions/.

12   Associated Press, "Policy Notifications and Current Status, by State," December 26, 2013, https://finance.yahoo.com/news/policy-notifications-current-status-state-204701399.html.

13   https://www.gofundme.com/coachwhite.

financial burden, which would've been greatly diminished if we had still had our previous plan, was overwhelming in the face of the diagnosis. That was pain inflicted on our family because of decisions made by politicians and bureaucrats in a distant city. That's not how things are supposed to be.[14]

The next time any liberal wants to lecture conservatives about helping people with pre-existing conditions, let him or her read this story. For that matter, let that person contribute to this GoFundMe page, which represents the only "coverage" one individual had after Obamacare bureaucrats snatched his insurance away.

Unfortunately, this story does not represent an isolated incident, as Obamacare's pre-existing condition provisions have literally priced millions out of coverage. The Kaiser Family Foundation noted that, from the first quarter of 2017 to the first quarter of 2018, more than 2.5 million individuals who do not qualify for Obamacare subsidies dropped their coverage.[15] Enrollment outside of the Obamacare exchanges dropped by 38%.[16] After a more than doubling of premiums from 2013 through 2017, a nearly 40% increase in rates for 2018 proved the last straw for many, and they dropped their coverage entirely.[17]

---

14   Jim White, personal communication, May 8, 2019.

15   Ashley Semanskee, Larry Levitt, and Cynthia Cox, "Data Note: Changes in Enrollment in the Individual Health Insurance Market," Kaiser Family Foundation, July 31, 2018, https://www.kff.org/health-reform/issue-brief/data-note-changes-in-enrollment-in-the-individual-health-insurance-market/.

16   Ibid.

17   HHS, "Data Point"; Department of Health and Human Services Office of Planning and Evaluation, "ASPE Research Brief: Health Plan Choice and Coverage in the 2018 Federal Health Insurance Exchange," October 30, 2017, https://aspe.hhs.gov/system/files/pdf/258456/Landscape_Master2018_1.pdf.

Despite all the political focus on pre-existing conditions, Americans care more about ensuring the affordability of their health-care coverage. Cato Institute polling demonstrates that the popularity of Obamacare's pre-existing condition provisions drops by 16 points when individuals are told that the provisions will increase premiums.[18] And a November 2018 Gallup survey found that, by double-digit margins, Americans care more about premium increases than whether they, or someone in their family, "will be denied health insurance coverage for a pre-existing medical condition."[19] Of course, liberal think-tanks won't conduct surveys asking whether the American people think the pre-existing condition provisions are worth higher premiums.[20]

But the more than 2.5 million individuals who dropped their insurance in a single year, likely because Obamacare's pre-existing condition provisions raised their premiums, have no coverage whatsoever should they suddenly develop a pre-existing condition. Therein lies the opportunity for conservatives. Whereas liberals want to ensure individuals have coverage *after* they develop a pre-existing condition, conservatives should focus on ensuring that people have coverage they can afford *before* they come down with a pre-existing condition, and can maintain after their diagnosis.

---

18   Emily Ekins, "The ACA's Pre-Existing Condition Regulations Lose Support When the Public Learns the Cost," Cato Institute, November 5, 2018, https://www.cato.org/survey-reports/acas-pre-existing-condition-regulations-lose-support-when-public-learns-cost.

19   Justin McCarthy, "Six in Ten Americans Worry About Higher Health Insurance Premiums," Gallup, December 10, 2018, https://news.gallup.com/poll/245312/six-americans-worry-higher-healthcare-premiums.aspx.

20   Jacobs, "What Liberals Won't Tell You About Pre-Existing Conditions," *The Federalist* June 28, 2018, https://thefederalist.com/2018/06/28/liberals-wont-tell-pre-existing-conditions/.

Obamacare articulates a one-size-fits-all approach to pre-existing conditions, requiring insurers to provide everyone with the same coverage. But that approach has literally priced millions out of the marketplace, leaving them to fend for themselves. Only repealing these regulations can relieve the millions of Americans struggling to afford coverage.

Instead of the sledgehammer that Obamacare took to insurance markets, conservatives should offer the proverbial scalpel, proposing a series of tailored solutions and options for patients regarding pre-existing conditions.[21] Those tailored solutions should focus on the first key principle of any sensible health reform.[22]

PRINCIPLE #1: PORTABLE, INDIVIDUAL INSURANCE

Liberal rhetoric about pre-existing conditions focuses on the symptoms—people unable to obtain coverage after they are diagnosed with serious, and costly, diseases—but ignores the underlying problem: Most Americans do not currently own their own health insurance. If individuals could buy, hold, and keep a policy for many years, if not their whole lifetime, then many fewer people would need to purchase coverage after developing a health condition.

Making insurance personally owned would not only reduce the pre-existing condition problem over time, it would also allow individuals, rather than their employers, to exercise greater

---

21   Chris Jacobs, "Four Better Ways to Address Pre-Existing Conditions Than Obamacare," *Federalist,* November 13, 2018, https://thefederalist.com/2018/11/13/4-better-ways-address-pre-existing-conditions-obamacare/.

22   Chris Jacobs, "Three Health Care Reforms Conservatives Should Rally Around," *Federalist,* December 4, 2018, https://thefederalist.com/2018/12/04/3-key-health-care-reforms-conservatives-rally-around/.

control over their health coverage and health care. Of course, it would also mean that government bureaucrats would have less of a role in health care, which might explain why the left spends most of its time micromanaging the symptoms rather than fixing the underlying problem.

These reforms would help to stave off the liberal march to single payer, by fixing the pre-existing condition problem in ways that put patients back in control.

Health Reimbursement Arrangements: A regulation the Trump administration proposed in 2018 could help to revolutionize the current health insurance system.[23] The proposed rule would allow employers to contribute money to Health Reimbursement Arrangements (HRAs), which individuals could use to fund their own health insurance tax-free.[24]

If adopted, this proposed rule would make health coverage individual and portable. Workers could purchase one health insurance policy, and keep it from job to job. Their employers would make a defined contribution—say, $500 per month—toward that policy through the HRA, and workers would pay any premium balance over and above the employer's contribution on a pre-tax basis.

Likewise, businesses would find this mechanism much

---

23 Chris Jacobs, "How an Obscure Regulatory Change Could Transform American Health Insurance," *The Federalist,* October 30, 2018, https://thefederalist. com/2018/10/30/how-an-obscure-regulatory-change-could-transform-american-health-insurance/.

24 Departments of the Treasury, Labor, and Health and Human Services, Proposed rule regarding "Health Reimbursement Arrangements and Other Account-Based Group Health Plans : A Proposed Rule" *Federal Register,* October 29, 2018, https://www.federalregister.gov/documents/2018/10/29/2018-23183/health-reimbursement-arrangements-and-other-account-based-group-health-plans pp. 54420–77.

simpler than the current menagerie of employer-provided health coverage. Firms could make predictable contributions to their workers' HRAs each month, making their costs easier to quantify. Employers could also forgo the administrative burden and expense of maintaining their own health plan, even as their workers would have many more insurance choices than most companies (particularly small businesses) can offer.

Health Status Insurance: Whereas HRAs could supplant the current system of employer-provided health insurance, health status insurance would complement it. Status insurance refers to the option for individuals to purchase coverage at some point in the future, should they need it. Put another way, these policies function as "health insurance insurance," guarding against a future pre-existing condition that might make an individual uninsurable.

Status insurance would guard against the classic pre-existing condition problem, whereby someone changes his job and can no longer obtain health coverage—or, worse yet, has to leave his job because of a health condition and loses his employment and coverage at the same time. At the time of their rollout just over a decade ago, status insurance policies cost one-fifth the amount of health insurance coverage.[25] At those prices, individuals could pay a few hundred dollars annually for the reassurance that, if they left their job, they would still have the ability to access quality, affordable coverage, by converting their status insurance into a full-fledged health plan.

Unfortunately, however, Obamacare's enactment made health status coverage obsolete. Reforming the federal insurance

---

25   Reed Abelson, "United to Insure the Right to Insurance," *New York Times*, December 2, 2008, https://www.nytimes.com/2008/12/03/business/03insure.html.

regulations to make status insurance a viable concept would provide protections for individuals who fear the diagnosis of a pre-existing condition—potentially at more affordable rates than the Obamacare *status quo*.

Other Reforms: Making health coverage portable would reduce the pre-existing condition problem over time. However, it would obviously not help those who already have pre-existing conditions, or individuals who develop pre-existing conditions early in life (e.g., congenital diseases). In those cases, state-based high-risk pools, with appropriate funding from the federal government, would provide coverage.

Policies about pre-existing conditions should also ensure that individuals can access quality care. For instance, direct primary care arrangements, which have grown in popularity in recent years, allow individuals to have frequent interactions with primary care doctors for a set monthly fee.[26] These arrangements could prove invaluable for individuals with chronic conditions, to help them to manage their care better.

Likewise, Harvard University professor Regina Herzlinger has promoted the concept of centers of excellence, which she called "focused factories," as a way to provide high-quality care to individuals with chronic conditions.[27] Because quality improves and cost often declines as hospitals perform more of a given type of procedure (e.g., heart bypass, knee replacement),

---

26   Lydia Ramsey, "A New Kind of Doctor's Office Charges a Monthly Fee and Doesn't Take Insurance—And It Could Be the Future of Medicine," *Business Insider,* March 19, 2017, https://www.businessinsider.com/direct-primary-care-a-no-insurance-healthcare-model-2017-3.

27   Regina Herzlinger, *Who Killed Health Care? America's $2 Trillion Medical Problem—And the Consumer-Driven Cure* (New York: McGraw-Hill, 2007), pp. 168-72.

patients would benefit by visiting high-volume facilities.

Walmart and other large employers have adopted this model for certain procedures, and have saved money while doing so, even after paying for patients' travel costs to visit the centers of excellence.[28] High-risk pools could provide a similar service for individuals with pre-existing conditions outside the employer marketplace.

At present, Obamacare does a disservice to individuals with pre-existing conditions. Because it requires insurers to accept all applicants, and charge applicants the same price regardless of health status, it encourages insurers to discriminate against sick patients. Small wonder then that few Obamacare insurers include prominent hospitals like the Mayo Clinic in their networks, because the law gives them every reason to avoid attracting sick patients.[29] Likewise, in 2014 a group of HIV patients filed a complaint against several Florida health insurers for failing to cover HIV drugs. The insurers placed all HIV/AIDS drugs, including generics, in the highest-cost tier, to discourage HIV-positive patients from applying for coverage.[30]

Reforms like high-risk pools, direct primary care, and centers of excellence would allow patients to receive quality

---

28   Lisa Woods, Jonathan Slotkin, and Ruth Coleman, "How Employers Are Fixing Health Care," *Harvard Business Review,* March 19, 2019, https://hbr.org/cover-story/2019/03/how-employers-are-fixing-health-care.

29   John Goodman, "Obamacare Can Be Worse Than Medicaid," *Wall Street Journal,* June 27, 2018, https://www.wsj.com/articles/obamacare-can-be-worse-than-medicaid-1530052891.

30   Michelle Andrews, "Complaint Says Insurance Plans Discriminate Against HIV Patients," NPR, July 8, 2014, https://www.npr.org/sections/health-shots/2014/07/08/329591574/complaint-says-insurance-plans-discriminate-against-hiv-patients.

care—and hopefully in ways that can lower the cost of care as well. They would help transform our current insurance system to focus on providing more personalized options to patients.

PRINCIPLE #2: A SUSTAINABLE SAFETY NET

The reasons for this reform principle seem obvious: $22 trillion in federal debt, and rising.[31] A Medicare program that needs shoring up, due to the retirement of 10,000 Baby Boomers each day.[32] More than $42 trillion in unfunded liabilities for the Medicare program over the next 75 years—more if one disregards the accounting gimmicks, and unrealistic payment reductions, included in Obamacare.[33]

Unfortunately, during the last presidential election, both major-party candidates saw fit to ignore the looming problems of America's entitlement system.[34] But politicians should not

---

31   Department of the Treasury, "The Debt to the Penny and Who Holds It," https://www.treasurydirect.gov/NP/debt/current.

32   Russell Heimlich, "Baby Boomers Retire," Pew Research Center, December 29, 2010, https://www.pewresearch.org/fact-tank/2010/12/29/baby-boomers-retire/.

33   Centers for Medicare and Medicaid Services, "2019 Annual Report of the Boards of Trustees of the Federal Hospital Insurance and Federal Supplemental Medical Insurance Trust Funds," April 22, 2019, https://www.cms.gov/Research-Statistics-Data-and-Systems/Statistics-Trends-and-Reports/ReportsTrustFunds/Downloads/TR2019.pdf?mod=article_inline, Table V.G1, Unfunded HI Obligations from Program Inception through the Infinite Horizon, p. 202, Table V.G3, Unfunded Part B Obligations from Program Inception through the Infinite Horizon, p. 204; and Table V.G5, Unfunded Part D Obligations from Program Inception through the Infinite Horizon, p. 206.

34   Chris Jacobs, "For Presidential Candidates, Some Inconvenient Truths on Entitlements," *National Review*, May 12, 2016, https://www.nationalreview.com/2016/05/medicare-insolvency-entitlement-crisis-2016-hillary-clinton-donald-trump-bernie-sanders/.

slough off the impending fiscal crisis, not least because financial markets may not allow them to do so.

At the heart of this reform principle lies the sentiment House Majority Leader Steny Hoyer (D-MD) expressed in 2009, and cited earlier in this book: "If we take care of everybody, we won't be able to take care of those who need us most."[35]

Liberals at times try to attack conservatives as uncaring, for wanting to set limits on government spending and intervention. But as Hoyer noted, trying to provide benefits to *everybody* could end up giving benefits to *nobody*—one of the prime downsides of a single-payer system. This principle understands the need for a safety net to protect the most vulnerable, but also sets clear priorities for that safety net, to make sure it can last for those truly in need.

Medicaid Reform: Obamacare's expansion of Medicaid coverage to the able-bodied has strained state and federal budgets alike. For states participating in expansion, enrollment has on average more than doubled beyond states' original projections.[36] The enrollment explosion has placed states under fiscal strain, as Medicaid continues to consume a larger and larger portion

---

35 Floor Remarks of Rep. Steny Hoyer on H.R. 3631, Medicare Premium Fairness Act of 2009, *Congressional Record* September 24, 2009, https://www.congress.gov/congressional-record/2009/09/24/house-section/article/H9908-1, pp. H9913-14.

36 Jonathan Ingram and Nicholas Horton, "Obamacare Expansion Enrollment Is Shattering Projections," Foundation for Government Accountability, November 16, 2016, https://thefga.org/download/ObamaCare-Expansion-is-Shattering-Projections.PDF, p. 5.

of their budgets.[37] One Democratic lawmaker in New Mexico admitted that, due to the rising cost of Medicaid expansion, "the most vulnerable of our citizens—the children, our senior citizens, our veterans, individuals with disabilities"—could "get hit."[38]

Just as important, Medicaid expansion places able-bodied adults ahead of the most vulnerable in our society, effectively discriminating against individuals with disabilities.[39] Obamacare gave states a 90% match to cover able-bodied adults, compared to only a 50-76% match to provide home care to individuals with disabilities.[40]

The 707,000 individuals with disabilities currently on Medicaid waiting lists for home and community-based care

---

37   Jonathan Ingram and Nicholas Horton, "A Budget Crisis in Three Parts: How Obamacare Is Bankrupting Taxpayers," Foundation for Government Accountability, February 1, 2018, https://thefga.org/wp-content/uploads/2018/02/A-Budget-Crisis-In-Three-Parts-2-6-18.pdf.

38   Christina Cassidy, "Rising Cost of Medicaid Expansion is Unnerving Some States," Associated Press, October 5, 2016, http://bigstory.ap.org/article/4219bc875f114b938 d38766c5321331a/rising-cost-medicaid-expansion-unnerving-some-states.

39   Chris Jacobs, "How Obamacare Undermines American Values: Penalizing Work, Citizenship, Marriage, and the Disabled," Heritage Foundation *Backgrounder No. 2862*, November 21, 2013, http://www.heritage.org/research/reports/2013/11/how-obamacare-undermines-american-values-penalizing-work-marriage-citizenship-and-the-disabled.

40   Section 2001(a) of the Patient Protection and Affordable Care Act, P.L. 111-148, codified at 42 U.S.C. 1396d(y)(1); Department of Health and Human Services, "Federal Matching Shares for Medicaid," *Federal Register,* November 21, 2017, https://www.govinfo.gov/content/pkg/FR-2017-11-21/pdf/2017-24953.pdf, Table 1, Federal Medical Assistance Percentages and Enhanced Federal Medical Assistance Percentages, Effective October 1, 2018-September 30, 2019, p. 55385.

should have priority over subsidies for able-bodied adults.[41] Sadly, however, since Obamacare's Medicaid expansion took effect, at least 21,904 individuals with disabilities in states that expanded Medicaid have died while on waiting lists for care.[42]

To right-size their budgets, and to end Obamacare's discrimination against individuals with disabilities, states and the federal government should freeze enrollment in Medicaid expansion.[43] Such a change would allow individuals currently on expansion to remain until they become ineligible, but states could not add any new individuals to the Medicaid rolls. In such a manner, states could reduce their rolls over time, as people move off public assistance and into work. This simple change would also save the federal government at least $525-$603 billion, and states at least $56-64 billion, over a decade.[44]

Once they have begun phasing out expansion, Congress should work with the states to provide additional flexibility for their Medicaid populations in exchange for a fixed-sum block

---

41 Kaiser Family Foundation, "Waiting List Enrollment for Medicaid Section 1915(c) Home and Community-Based Services Waivers," April 2019, https://www.kff.org/health-reform/state-indicator/waiting-lists-for-hcbs-waivers/?currentTimeframe=0&sortModel=%7B%22colId%22:%22Location%22,%22sort%22:%22asc%22%7D.

42 Nicholas Horton, "Waiting for Help: The Medicaid Waiting List Crisis," Foundation for Government Accountability, March 6, 2018, https://thefga.org/wp-content/uploads/2018/03/WAITING-FOR-HELP-The-Medicaid-Waiting-List-Crisis-07302018.pdf.

43 Chris Jacobs, "Putting Obamacare in a Deep Freeze," *National Review*, December 7, 2016, http://www.nationalreview.com/article/442820/obamacare-repeal-replace-enrollment-freeze-first-step.

44 Foundation for Government Accountability, "Freezing Medicaid Expansion Enrollment Will Save Taxpayers More Than Half a Trillion," February 2017, https://thefga.org/wp-content/uploads/2017/02/MedEx-Freeze-Savings-Table.pdf.

grant. Rhode Island agreed to a similar arrangement under the Bush administration in January 2009, in which the state received expanded waiver authority from federal regulations in exchange for a capped level of federal funding.

The success of Rhode Island's Medicaid reform provides a way forward for other states. In Rhode Island, per-beneficiary spending declined over a five-year period, and overall spending in Medicaid remained flat for four years, even as enrollment in the program increased during the Great Recession.[45] Rhode Island lowered spending on Medicaid not by stinting on care, but providing more of it—better coordinating care and providing more primary care, particularly for vulnerable patients.[46] The Rhode Island model provides a clear example of how Medicaid reform can present a "win-win" opportunity, in which taxpayers can save money *and* patients can receive better care—with the former occurring because of the latter.

Medicare Reform: Absent Obamacare's deceptive double-counting, whereby Democrats credited provisions as both funding the law's coverage expansions and extending Medicare's solvency, the Part A (Hospital Insurance) Trust Fund would likely have faced insolvency.[47] Put another way, the current

---

45   Testimony of Gary Alexander, former Rhode Island secretary of Health and Human Services, on "Strengthening Medicaid Long-Term Supports and Services" before the Commission on Long Term Care, August 1, 2013, http://ltccommission.org/ltccommission/wp-content/uploads/2013/12/Garo-Alexander.pdf. The author served as a member of the Commission.

46   Lewin Group, "An Independent Evaluation of Rhode Island's Global Waiver," December 6, 2011, http://www.ohhs.ri.gov/documents/documents11/Lewin_report_12_6_11.pdf.

47   Jacobs, "Some Inconvenient Truths."

Medicare program is already functionally insolvent; Obamacare's accounting gimmicks merely masked the problem from the public, and allowed Washington politicians to avoid the issue. While the program desperately needs reform, two solutions could go a long way toward solving Medicare's shortfalls—if politicians have the courage to act.

First, lawmakers should reform the Medicare benefit, introducing a combined deductible for Part A (hospital coverage) and Part B (physician coverage) of traditional Medicare, while reforming Medigap supplemental coverage. This reform would create a cap on out-of-pocket expenses, which does not currently exist in traditional Medicare. It would also save four out of five Medigap policy-holders an average of $415 per year, by reducing the need for seniors to spend money on expensive supplemental insurance coverage.[48]

Congress should also convert Medicare into a system that provides seniors a generous contribution to purchase an insurance plan of their choosing—whether a private plan or traditional Medicare—to deliver their benefits. The Congressional Budget Office concluded in 2017 that one such mechanism would save the federal government $184 billion, while *also* reducing seniors' premiums by 7%, and their total out-of-pocket spending by 5%.[49]

---

48 Kaiser Family Foundation, "Medigap Reforms: Potential Effects of Benefit Restrictions on Medicare Spending and Beneficiary Costs," July 2011, https://www.kff.org/wp-content/uploads/2013/01/8208.pdf, Exhibit 2, Changes in Medicare Spending per Beneficiary and Average Beneficiary Costs under Three Medigap Benefit Options, p. 6.

49 Congressional Budget Office, "A Premium Support System for Medicare: Updated Analysis of Alternative Options," October 5, 2017, https://www.cbo.gov/system/files/115th-congress-2017-2018/reports/53077-premiumsupport.pdf. Estimates cited refer to CBO's average bid option for calculating premium support payments, without grandfathering in existing beneficiaries.

This premium support system represents the ultimate "win-win" proposition, in which both seniors and taxpayers benefit. It can do so by unleashing the benefits of competition among private plans and traditional Medicare. It will help make our current Medicare system more sustainable by properly aligning incentives within one key portion of our health-care system.

PRINCIPLE #3: PROPERLY ALIGNING INCENTIVES

The ongoing discussion about whether our country spends too much, or too little, on health care misses one key point. At present, our health-care system costs so much because it contains skewed incentives. To put it bluntly, Americans do a good job of spending everyone else's money, which helps to explain why costs continue to rise ever higher.

A better system would focus on making it possible for Americans to spend more of their own money, which would promote both transparency and efficiency throughout health care markets. If Americans had more properly aligned incentives, and chose to increase their spending on health care, that will represent millions of rational choices by individuals. On the other hand, aligning the incentives correctly could result in lower health costs, if it makes waste in the system more readily apparent.

Tax Treatment of Health Insurance: The current tax treatment of health insurance creates several problems. First, because the federal tax code excludes employer-sponsored coverage, but not individually purchased insurance, from both payroll and income taxes, workers have a strong incentive to obtain coverage from their employers. That employer-based coverage creates the portability problems—and the pre-existing condition problems—outlined above.

Second, the federal tax code provides no limit to the

exclusion for employer-sponsored health coverage. Under current law, individuals pay anywhere from 30-50% of their wages in federal and state income and payroll taxes, but no tax at all on health coverage, no matter how generous. Most economists agree that this provision encourages individuals to over-consume health insurance, and ultimately health care.[50]

A better solution would impose a standard deduction for health coverage, available to those with employer-sponsored coverage and who buy health insurance on their own. If households purchase coverage valued below the amount of the standard deduction, they would receive an added tax benefit compared to current law.

For instance, assume this proposal sets the standard deduction set at $20,000 for family coverage. If a family buys a plan with a premium of only $15,000 per year, they would still get to write off the full $20,000 standard deduction for health coverage on their taxes, whereas at present, they would only receive a tax benefit based on the $15,000 value of their plan.

The standard deduction would better align incentives in two respects. The prospect of an added tax benefit would encourage individuals to spend wisely when shopping for health coverage in the short term. In the longer term, growing the value of the deduction at a slower rate—for instance, the rate of overall inflation, rather than the (higher) rate of health-care inflation—would help reverse rising health-care costs.

Health Savings Accounts: HSAs represent one way to change the tax treatment of health insurance, by encouraging individuals

---

50   Congressional Budget Office, "Key Issues in Analyzing Major Health Insurance Proposals," December 18, 2008, https://www.cbo.gov/sites/default/files/110th-congress-2007-2008/reports/12-18-keyissues.pdf, pp. 85-87.

to save for medical expenses in a pre-tax account. They have proven popular with many American families, with at least 21.8 million individuals purchasing HSA-eligible coverage, and HSA account balances set to hit $75 billion by the end of 2020.[51]

Ideal reforms would increase the annual limit on contributions to an HSA, and allow HSA funds to pay for health insurance premiums. Like the Health Reimbursement Arrangement provision discussed above, this change would make health coverage more portable, by allowing employers to make contributions to workers' accounts that workers can then use to purchase health insurance. Unlike HRAs, however, HSA funds belong to individuals and not employers, so allowing HSAs to pay for premiums would make both the insurance coverage and leftover fund balances portable to employees.

Scope of Practice: States also have a role to play in aligning incentives properly. They can start by ensuring that medical professionals, like nurse practitioners, can work to the highest scope of their medical training. Currently, some states impose additional restrictions on practitioners—requiring direct supervision by physicians, for instance—that many experts consider unnecessary.[52]

With our nation facing a physician shortage, reforming

---

51   America's Health Insurance Plans, "Health Savings Accounts and Consumer-Directed Health Plans Grow as Valuable Financial Planning Tools," April 12, 2018, https://www.ahip.org/wp-content/uploads/2018/04/HSA_Report_4.12.18-1.pdf; Devenir Research, "2018 Year-End HSA Market Statistics and Trends Executive Summary," February 27, 2019, http://www.devenir.com/wp-content/uploads/2018-Year-End-Devenir-HSA-Research-Report-Executive-Summary.pdf.

52   Institute of Medicine, "The Future of Nursing: Focus on Scope of Practice," *Report Brief*, October 2010, http://www.iom.edu/~/media/Files/Report%20Files/2010/The-Future-of-Nursing/Nursing%20Scope%20of%20Practice%202010%20Brief.pdf.

scope of practice laws can improve access to care, particularly in rural and underserved areas.[53] Scope of practice can also help control the growth of health-care costs, both by expanding available supply and by providing more appropriate service venues—for instance, treating a knee sprain at an urgent care center rather than the emergency room.

Certificate of Need: Here again, state reforms can help improve access to care. Many states have laws that require entities seeking to construct new facilities—from hospitals to MRI clinics to nursing homes—to obtain approval from a government board (i.e., a certificate of need) before doing so. Of course, these boards provide an opportunity for existing providers to keep out potential competition by urging the boards to deny any newcomers the certificate they need to operate.

Certificate of need laws have their roots in a 1970s-style approach to health care that uses centralized planning by bureaucrats to substitute for the judgment of individual patients and doctors. However, research indicates that these laws do not restrain health costs or improve quality.[54] Rather than using the edicts of a government board to control health costs, states should instead repeal their certificate of need laws, and focus on reforming other incentives in the health-care system to make it function more efficiently.

---

53   IHS Markit, "The Complexities of Physician Supply and Demand: Projections from 2016 to 2030," Report for the American Association of Medical Colleges, March 2018, https://aamc-black.global.ssl.fastly.net/production/media/filer_public/85/d7/85d7b689-f417-4ef0-97fb-ecc129836829/aamc_2018_workforce_projections_update_april_11_2018.pdf.

54   Matthew Mitchell, "Certificate of Need Laws: Are They Achieving Their Goals?" Mercatus Center, August 2017, https://www.mercatus.org/system/files/mitchell-con-qa-mop-mercatus-v2.pdf.

The above concepts represent just some of the better alternatives to our current health-care problems and to a government-run, single-payer health system. Most importantly, they put patients at the center of the system, rather than constructing a new bureaucratic apparatus and hoping patients ultimately benefit from it.

Conservatives need to make the case for these better ideas, even as they make the case against single payer. The American people deserve better than the broken status quo, and than single payer. By making sound arguments on both fronts, conservatives can deliver on the former, and prevent the latter.

conclusion

If September 13, 2017—the date on which Sen. Bernie Sanders re-introduced his single-payer legislation—provides one turning point illustrating the hard left turn of the Democratic Party, the coming months may bring another. The American people will have an opportunity to weigh in on two very different visions of health care.

As we have seen throughout this volume, government-run health care ends up harming the people who need care the most:

- Medicaid patients who cannot access physicians

- Individuals with disabilities waiting literally years for home-based care—and in some cases dying before receiving it—

while states instead decide to expand Medicaid to able-bodied adults

- Patients in Canada who must literally wait months for treatment

- British residents who cannot obtain treatments bureaucrats deem too costly

- The sickest Americans, who face discrimination by insurers because Obamacare encourages them to shun costly patients

The massive tax increases, federal regulation, and government spending accompanying single payer—all of which will bankrupt the economy, and future generations of Americans—provide reason enough for the American people to reject the push for socialized medicine.

But the way government-run health care especially harms those in greatest need of assistance shows the moral bankruptcy of this approach. Single payer would leave vulnerable patients with a crowded, and likely under-funded, federal health system, and few if any options to obtain care outside it.

Conservatives can, and must, make the argument against socialized medicine. But they must also make the argument in favor of a better alternative. Thankfully, single payer provides a helpful contrast to the conservative approach—one that moves toward coverage owned and controlled by individuals, not employers or government bureaucrats, and puts patients and doctors at the heart of medicine, not regulatory diktats from Washington.

Hopefully, this book has helped to illuminate a better path forward. The American people deserve better than single-payer health care. Once educated about all its harmful effects, they should demand it.

APPENDIX: SECTION-BY-SECTION ANALYSIS OF H.R. 1384 AND S. 1129, MEDICARE FOR ALL ACT OF 2019

Because the House legislation is longer (120 pages) and somewhat more detailed than the Senate version (100 pages), the below analysis summarizes the House bill. Major differences between the House and Senate bills are summarized in italics.

TITLE I—ESTABLISHMENT OF THE PROGRAM; COVERAGE; ENROLLMENT

Section 101—Establishment

Establishes a "national health insurance program to provide comprehensive protection against the costs of health care and health-related services."

Section 102—Universal Coverage

Makes "every individual who is a resident of the United States" eligible for benefits. Allows the secretary of Health and Human Services (HHS) to make "other individuals" eligible for benefits, "to ensure that every person in the

United States has access to health care," while preventing individuals from traveling "for the sole purpose of obtaining health care" services.

Section 103—Freedom of Choice

Allows any individual entitled to benefits to receive those benefits from "any institution, agency, or individual qualified to participate" in the program.

Section 104—Non-Discrimination

Prevents any individual from being denied benefits from, or the opportunity to participate in, the program based on "race, color, national origin, age, disability…or sex, including sex stereotyping, gender identity, sexual orientation, and pregnancy and related medical conditions (including termination of pregnancy)." Requires the secretary to establish a procedure for investigating such complaints administratively, and allows aggrieved individuals to file claims in any federal district court.

Section 105—Enrollment

Requires the secretary to provide a mechanism to enroll individuals in the program, and issue "Universal Medicare card[s]" for identification and claims processing. The cards shall not include beneficiaries' Social Security numbers.

Section 106—Effective Date of Benefits

Makes benefits available two years after the date of enactment. Individuals younger than age 19 or older than age 55 one year after enactment may receive benefits at that time; however, they may continue in their existing coverage for a one-year transition period until the entire program takes effect (i.e., two years after enactment).

The Senate bill includes a four-year transition, rather than a two-year transition. Only individuals younger than age 19 would become eligible early, effective on January 1 of the first year after enactment. Other individuals could buy into the program, as outlined in Sections 1001 and 1002 of the Senate bill.

Section 107—Prohibition Against Duplicating Coverage

Beginning on the effective date, makes it unlawful for a private insurer to sell, or an employer to offer, coverage that "duplicates the benefits provided" under the act. Permits "the sale of health insurance coverage for any additional benefits not covered" by the act.

TITLE II—COMPREHENSIVE COVERAGE

Section 201—Comprehensive Benefits

Makes individuals "entitled to have payment made…to an eligible provider for the following items and services if medically necessary":

1. "Hospital services, including inpatient and outpatient hospital care, including 24-hour-a-day emergency services and inpatient prescription drugs";

2. "Ambulatory patient services";

3. "Primary and preventive services, including chronic disease management";

4. "Prescription drugs and medical devices, including outpatient prescription drugs, medical devices, and biological products";

5. "Mental health and substance abuse treatment services, including inpatient care;"

6. "Laboratory and diagnostic services";

7. "Comprehensive reproductive, maternity, and newborn care";

8. "Pediatrics";

9. "Oral health, audiology, and vision services";

10. "Rehabilitative and habilitative services and devices";

11. "Emergency services and transportation";

12. "Early and periodic screening, diagnostic, and treatment services";

13. "Necessary transportation to receive health care services for persons with disabilities or low-income individuals"; and

14. "Long-term care services and support," as described in Section 204 below.

Requires the secretary to evaluate and update the list of services at least annually, and make recommendations to Congress. Also requires the secretary to consult with experts in "complementary and alternative medicine" about whether and how to include such practices in single payer.

Permits states to provide additional benefits for their residents, and provide benefits to individuals not eligible for benefits, at their own expense.

The Senate bill covers all the benefits outlined above, except long-term services and supports. With respect to these services, the Senate bill covers only home and community-based services as part of the federal program. State Medicaid programs would continue to provide institutional care, as outlined in Section 204 below.

Section 202—No Cost-Sharing

Prohibits the imposition of any "cost-sharing, including deductibles, co-insurance, co-payments, or similar charges." Also prohibits providers from charging enrolled individuals for services provided under the act.

The Senate bill permits cost-sharing for "prescription drugs and biological products" only, up to an annual maximum of $200 per person per year. The cost-sharing would not apply to preventive drugs, or to any individual with a household income less than 200% of the federal poverty level ($51,500 for a family of four in 2019).

Section 203—Exclusions and Limitations   Requires covered goods and services to meet regulations the secretary sets. Requires the secretary to make national coverage determinations regarding experimental treatments, and to create an appeals process for coverage decisions.

Allows HHS to establish national practice guidelines, in which case items and services provided under those guidelines shall be considered eligible for coverage. Allows individual providers to override such national standards, if using appropriate professional judgment in the best interest of the patient.

Section 204—Coverage of Long-Term Care Services

Creates an entitlement for coverage of long-term supports and services for any mental or physical condition that "causes a functional limitation in performing one or more activities of daily living," such as eating, bathing, and dressing, or "requires a similar need of assistance in performing instrumental activities of daily living," such as managing finances and conducting chores, "due to cognitive or other impairments." Requires the secretary to develop a process for determining individuals' eligibility and assessing their needed services.

Describes criteria for covered services, which shall include "a broad spectrum of long-term services and supports." Prioritizes home and community-based services over institutionalization in nursing homes, and states that individuals will receive community-based services "unless an individual elects otherwise." Requires the secretary to consult with an advisory commission when determining the covered services.

The Senate bill would maintain coverage of institutional long-term care services—such as nursing-home care and inpatient psychiatric care—through state Medicaid programs. State Medicaid programs would cover institutional long-term care only, and would no longer cover other services, such as home and community-based care or health-care services (e.g., doctor and hospital visits, etc.), which would be provided through the new federal program.

The Senate bill includes maintenance of effort provisions regarding state Medicaid coverage of institutional long-term care. States cannot reduce their eligibility standards below those in place as of January 1, 2019. States must also maintain their spending levels for Medicaid institutional long-term services, calculated based on spending levels in fiscal year 2018 and updated for inflation by an adjustment factor calculated by the secretary.

The Senate bill includes a Section 205, prohibiting state Medicaid programs from imposing liens against the estates of individuals who received nursing-home benefits, "except pursuant to the judgement of a court on account of benefits incorrectly paid."

The Senate bill includes a Section 206, permitting states to set their own additional standards, "provided that such standards do not restrict eligibility or reduce access to services."

TITLE III—PROVIDER PARTICIPATION

Section 301—Provider Participation and Standards; Whistleblower Protections

Requires providers furnishing services covered under the act to file participation agreements. In the participation agreements, providers shall agree to provide services without discrimination and without cost-sharing to patients, not to employ "any individual or other provider that has had a participation agreement...terminated for cause," provide proper documentation of services rendered, and comply with other requirements.

Providers must ensure "that no board member, executive, or administrator of [an institutional] provider receives compensation from, owns stock or has other financial investments in, or serves as a board member of any entity that contracts with or provides items or services, including pharmaceutical products and medical devices or equipment, to such provider." *The Senate bill does not include this provision.*

States that "each health care provider...has a duty to advocate for and to act in the exclusive interest of each individual...such that no financial interest or relationship impairs any health care provider's ability to furnish necessary and appropriate care." Requires the secretary to pass reporting rules that will "prohibit participating providers, spouses, and immediate family members of participating providers, from accepting or entering into any arrangement for any bonus, incentive payment, profit-sharing, or compensation based on patient utilization or based on financial outcomes," or from serving as board members for or receiving any compensation from a contractor to that provider. *The Senate bill does not include these provisions.*

Allows for termination of participation agreements, whether by the secretary, by the provider, or as a result of a conviction for fraudulent activity. Requires "notice and a reasonable opportunity to correct deficiencies before the secretary terminates an agreement," unless "public safety or similar reasons" require a faster termination.

Prohibits the secretary from terminating the participation of, "or in any other way discriminat[ing] against," a provider for bringing information to state or federal authorities regarding violations of the act, or "refusing to participate in, any activity, policy, practice, or assigned task that the provider or representative reasonably believes to be in violation of any provision" of the act, or any rule promulgated under the act.

Prohibits any person from "discharg[ing] or otherwise discriminat[ing]" against an employee for notifying the employer, or state or federal authorities, about alleged wrongdoing. Provides for a private right of action, subject to the statute of limitations laid out in the False Claims Act, for any individual alleging discrimination by an employer. *The Senate bill does not include these provisions.*

Section 302—Qualifications for Providers

Provides that a health-care provider is qualified to furnish covered items and services if certified or licensed in compliance with state law, and any applicable federal requirements. States that "any provider qualified to provide health-care items and services through the Department of Veterans Affairs or Indian Health Service is a qualifying provider" for individuals who qualify for those services.

Requires the secretary to create national minimum standards under the act, which may include such elements as facility adequacy, training and competence, performance standards, and outcomes. *The House bill, but not the Senate bill, includes an additional provision allowing for the creation of "mandatory minimum safe registered nurse to patient staffing ratios and optimal staffing levels for physicians and other health care practitioners."*

Section 303—Use of Private Contracts

Prohibits participating providers from contracting privately for any covered service. Permits participating providers to contract privately for non-covered services, provided the patient signs a written contract not entered into "when the individual is facing an emergency health care situation," and that the provider files an affidavit with the secretary stating that the provider will not submit a claim to the federal program for such services.

If the provider "knowingly and willfully" submits a claim for such services, "or receives any reimbursement or amount for any such item or service," the contract is null and void, "no payment shall be made under this title for any item or service furnished by the provider" for a one-year period, and "any payment received...for any item or service furnished during such period shall be remitted."

Participating providers may contract privately with any individuals not eligible for the single-payer program for any service. Non-participating providers may contract privately with eligible individuals, provided the patient signs a written contract not entered into "when the individual is facing an emergency health care situation," and that the provider files an affidavit with the secretary stating that the provider "will not submit any claim...for any covered item or service" for two years.

If the provider "knowingly and willfully" submits a claim to the federal program for such services, "or receives any reimbursement or amount for any such item or service," the contract is null and void, "no payment shall be made under this title for any item or service furnished by the provider" for a two-year period, and "any payment received...for any item or service furnished during such period shall be remitted."

The Senate bill includes similar provisions, except that providers who contract privately cannot bill the new program for one year, whereas the House legislation would prohibit non-participating providers who contract privately with eligible individuals from billing the government program for two years.

TITLE IV—ADMINISTRATION

Section 401—Administration

Provides the general duties of the secretary in implementing the act, including related to eligibility; enrollment; benefits provided; provider participation criteria; levels of funding; determining payment methods; making coverage determinations; planning for capital expenditures; planning for workforce education funding; encouraging states to develop regional planning mechanisms; and "any other regulations necessary to carry out the purposes of this Act." *The House bill, but not the Senate bill, also gives the secretary "the obligation to ensure the timely and accessible provision of items and services that all eligible individuals are entitled to" under the act.*

Requires the secretary to "ensure an adequate national database" relating to health services and costs, including patient outcomes. *The House bill, but not the Senate bill, includes more specific language regarding the database, requiring participating providers to disclose all data presently required by government programs (e.g., the current Medicare and Medicaid programs), along with "annual financial data that includes information on employees (including the number of employees, hours worked, and wage information) by job title and by each patient care unit or department within each facility (including outpatient units or departments); the number of registered nurses per staffed bed by each such unit or department; information on the dollar value and annual spending (including purchases, upgrades, and maintenance) for health information technology; and risk-adjusted and raw patient outcome data (including data on medical, surgical, obstetric, and other procedures)."*

Requires the secretary to analyze the data, and issue regulations permitting its release for research purposes (with patient identifying information removed). Requires the secretary to submit annual reports to Congress regarding the act, including implementation, enrollment, benefits, cost-containment measures, health disparities, and opportunities for improvement.

Permits the secretary to commission studies, and "develop and test methods...as the Secretary may consider necessary or promising for the evaluation, or for the improvement, of the operation of this Act." Requires the Government Accountability Office to audit the program every five years.

Section 402—Consultation

Requires the secretary to consult with "federal agencies, Indian tribes and urban Indian health organizations, and private entities, such as labor organizations representing health care workers, professional societies, national associations, nationally recognized associations of health care experts, medical schools and academic health centers, consumer groups, and business organizations...to ensure the broadest and most informed input in the administration of this Act."

Section 403—Regional Administration

Requires the secretary to establish regional offices to "promot[e] adequate access to, and efficient use of, tertiary care facilities, equipment, and services" by beneficiaries. Each regional office shall have a director appointed by the secretary, and a deputy director to represent Indian and Alaska Native tribes in the region, if any. Where possible, the regions should incorporate existing Centers for Medicare and Medicaid Services (CMS) regional offices. Each office shall prepare an annual needs assessment, recommend changes in provider reimbursement or payment, and establish quality assurance mechanisms in each region.

Section 404—Beneficiary Ombudsman

Requires the secretary to appoint a beneficiary ombudsman to receive complaints from, and provide assistance to, individuals dissatisfied with elements of the program, and submit annual reports to Congress and the secretary on beneficiary complaints. "The Ombudsman shall not serve as an advocate for any increases in payments or new coverage of services, but may identify issues and problems in payment or coverage policies."

Section 405—Conduct of Related Health Programs

With respect to other programs in the Department of Health and Human Services' remit (e.g., disability insurance, health personnel education and research), requires the secretary to "direct the activities of the Department...toward contributions to the health of the people complementary to this Act."

Section 411—Application of Federal Sanctions to All Fraud and Abuse Under the Medicare for All Program

Extends a series of existing anti-fraud provisions that apply to the current Medicare and Medicaid programs to the new program, including provisions related to 1) the exclusion of individuals and entities (i.e., medical providers) from the program; 2) civil monetary penalties; 3) criminal penalties; 4) disclosure of ownership and related information; 5) disclosure of certain owners previously excluded from the programs for fraud-related offenses; and 6) physician self-referral.

TITLE V—QUALITY ASSESSMENT

Section 501—Quality Standards

Requires CMS's Center for Clinical Standards and Quality, in coordination with the Agency for Healthcare Research and Quality (AHRQ), to implement and evaluate all standards and quality measures. Requires the Center for Clinical

Standards to review and evaluate all existing AHRQ research, and determine which standards are appropriate to incorporate as national practice guidelines. Requires the center to submit a report annually to the secretary about practice guidelines, which "may affect the Secretary's determination of coverage of services."

The House bill, but not the Senate bill, includes additional language prohibiting "the use of Quality-Adjusted Life Years, Disability-Adjusted Life Years, or other similar mechanisms that discriminate against people with disabilities…in any value or cost-effectiveness assessments."

Section 502—Addressing Health Care Disparities

Requires the Center for Clinical Standards to evaluate the collection of data "on disparities in health care services and performance on the basis of race, ethnicity, gender, geography…or socioeconomic status." Requires the center to regularly report to Congress and the secretary on ways to collect and evaluate data on health disparities, and requires the secretary to implement changes the reports identify.

TITLE VI—HEALTH BUDGET; PAYMENTS; COST CONTAINMENT MEASURES

Section 601—National Health Budget

Requires the secretary to submit a national health budget by September 1 each year. The budget would consist of eight components: 1) an operating budget; 2) a capital expenditures budget; 3) a special projects budget for health professional shortage areas; 4) quality assessment activities; 5) health professional education; 6) administrative costs; 7) a reserve fund to respond to emergencies (e.g., a pandemic);

and 8) prevention and public health activities.

Allows the secretary to allocate the national health budget among the components, and directs the secretary to provide each regional office "with an allotment the Secretary determines appropriate" to carry out the act in each region.

For "up to five years" after the program's enactment, allocates "at least one percent of the budget...to programs providing assistance to workers who perform functions in the administration of the health insurance system, or related functions within health care institutions or organizations... who may experience economic dislocation" as a result of the act's implementation.

The Senate bill includes a slightly different description of the national health budget components, contains no specific provision for allocating the budget to various regions, and provides for "up to one percent" of the budget to be used for transitional worker assistance, as opposed to "at least one percent."

Section 611—Payments to Institutional Providers Based on Global Budget

Requires the secretary to provide quarterly lump-sum payments to institutional providers (including hospitals and nursing homes), which shall constitute payment in full for all inpatient and outpatient services rendered. Group physician practices and other related health-care providers can elect to join a facility's global budget, provided those physicians are paid on a salaried basis.

The regional director will "negotiate" the amount of the payment with the provider, and review the adequacy of the payments quarterly, considering "additional funding necessary for unanticipated items and services," changes in market conditions, and the need for any adjustments. The current Medicare prospective payment system shall serve as the initial baseline for the negotiations, except that the new system "shall not include…value-based payment adjustments" and adjustments for capital expenses (considered separately in the capital expenditures section below).

Global payment levels will consider historical volumes of services provided; actual expenditures at the facility compared to those of other facilities; projected changes in services; employee wages, including any needed to meet required staff-to-patient ratios; the provider's maximum capacity; education and prevention; and "any other factor determined appropriate by the Secretary." Payment amounts may not take into account capital expenditures, exceed the provider's capacity to provide services, or compensate directors or executives with financial conflicts of interest.

Operating expenses will include wages and salaries for all staff, costs for all pharmaceuticals and medical devices dispensed within the facility, patient care and education, incidental services, and administrative costs. Providers may not pay any employees more than the compensation caps set in federal law. *The Senate bill does not include this section, nor any provision regarding global budgets for hospitals and nursing homes.*

Section 612—Payment to Individual Providers through Fee-for-Service

Requires the secretary to establish a physician fee schedule one year after enactment, and update it annually. The fee schedule will take into account the existing physician fee schedule under the current Medicare program, and "the expertise of providers and value of items and services furnished by such providers." Payment will apply to all doctors, except those group practices using the global payment method above, and will constitute payment in full, with additional charges to patients prohibited.

Requires each regional director to establish a physician practice review board "to assure quality, cost effectiveness, and fair reimbursements" for physician services. "The use of Quality Adjusted Life Years, Disability-Adjusted Life Years, or other similar mechanisms that discriminate against people with disabilities is prohibited for use in any value or cost-effectiveness assessments."

The Senate bill includes a Section 611 providing for fee schedules for both hospitals and physicians "consistent with the process for determining payments for items and services" under the current Medicare program. The section also applies existing Medicare payment demonstration projects to the new single-payer program. The section does not contain language included in the House bill prohibiting the use of Quality Adjusted Life Years and related metrics.

Section 613—Ensuring Accurate Valuation of Services under the Medicare Physician Fee Schedule

Effective one year after enactment, requires a "standardized process for reviewing the relative values of physicians' services." Requires the secretary to submit to Congress a plan for tracking relative values, such as via a database. Requires a review of "potentially misvalued" codes every year, and a full review of all codes every four years (as opposed to five under current law).

Also requires the secretary to consult with the Medicare

Payment Advisory Commission on adjustments to billing codes. Requires the Government Accountability Office to audit the secretary's process for adjusting billing codes "periodically." *The Senate bill includes this section as Section 612.*

Section 614—Payment Prohibitions; Capital Expenditures; Special Projects

Includes "Sense of Congress" language stating that "tens of millions of people in the United States do not receive health care services while billions of dollars that could be spent on providing health care are diverted to profit. There is a moral imperative to correct the massive deficiencies in our current health system and to eliminate profit from the provision of health care."

Prohibits payments to providers from taking into account, or being used by a provider for 1) marketing; 2) profit or net revenue; 3) "incentive payments, bonuses, or other compensation based on patient utilization of items and services...including any value-based payment or employment-based compensation;" 4) payments to labor relations consultants to educate employees about whether to join a union; and 5) prohibited political campaign contributions.

Instructs the secretary to pay from the capital expenditure budget "such sums determined appropriate by the Secretary," with priority going to funds improving service in medically underserved areas or to address health-care disparities. Prohibits any funding of capital projects "that results in care reductions to patients, including reductions in registered nursing staffing patterns and changes in emergency room or primary care services or availability."

Prohibits institutional providers from using "operating

expenses and funds…for a capital project funded by charitable donations" without the approval of the relevant regional director or directors. Prohibits providers from using funds designated for operating expenses for capital expenses or profit, or using funds for capital expenses for operating costs.

Requires the secretary to grant to each regional director "such sums determined appropriate" for special projects, including for facilities in underserved or health professional shortage areas. Prohibits the secretary from "utiliz[ing] any quality metrics or standards" when determining provider payment methodologies. *The Senate bill does not include this section or any of its provisions.*

Section 615—Office of Primary Health Care
Establishes this office within the Agency for Healthcare Research and Quality, to coordinate health education goals, promote training for primary care practitioners, and consult on the special projects component of the national health budget. Within one year of enactment, requires the office to "set forth national goals to increase access to high quality primary health care." *The Senate bill includes this section as Section 613.*

Section 616—Payments for Prescription Drugs and Approved Devices and Equipment
Requires the secretary to "negotiate" prices for drugs and medical devices. The secretary must consider "the comparative clinical effectiveness and cost effectiveness," budgetary impact, similarly effective or alternative therapies, a manufacturer's total revenues, and "associated investment in research and development of such drug."

Provides that "in the case that the Secretary is unable to

successfully negotiate an appropriate price" for a drug, the secretary "shall authorize the use of any patent...or other exclusivity granted by the federal government with respect to such drug as the Secretary determines appropriate for purposes of manufacturing such drug for sale." Provides that other entities using a competitive license shall provide to the original manufacturer "reasonable compensation, as determined by the Secretary" based on 1) any federal subsidies used to develop the drug, 2) the value of investment made by the manufacturer to develop the drug, 3) "the impact of the price...on meeting the medical need of all patients at a reasonable cost," 4) "the relationship between the price of such drug" and its health benefits, and 5) any other factors considered by the secretary. Manufacturers "may seek recovery against the United States" in the Court of Federal Claims.

If the secretary decides to license competitors to a branded drug, the price for its first year shall consist of the average price in the ten largest Organization for Economic Cooperation and Development (OECD) countries, as determined by gross domestic product.

Prioritizes Food and Drug Administration (FDA) review of any entity the secretary grants a license to produce prescription drugs. Prohibits drug manufacturers from "anti-competitive behavior" that "interfere[s] with the issuance and implementation of a competitive license or run[s] contrary to public policy." Grants the secretary the authority to require drug manufacturers "to disclose... such information that the Secretary determines necessary" to carry out the licensing provisions.

The Senate bill includes this section as Section 614 of the bill. The Senate bill directs the secretary to negotiate drug and device prices annually, and establish a formulary that will promote the use of generics "to the greatest extent possible." In addition, the formulary "shall encourage best practices in prescribing and discourage the use of ineffective, dangerous, or excessively costly medications when better alternatives are available." The Senate bill does not include any provision allowing the secretary to license off pharmaceutical patents.

TITLE VII—UNIVERSAL MEDICARE TRUST FUND

Section 701—Universal Medicare Trust Fund

Creates the new trust fund in the Treasury, which shall consist of "such gifts and bequests as may be made and such amounts as many be deposited in, or appropriated to," the fund.

Appropriates money into the fund every year equal to the tax revenue generated from 1) the prohibition on employer coverage of health benefits (which employers can currently provide on a pre-tax basis) under the new program and 2) repeal of the exchange (i.e., Obamacare) premium subsidies.

For the program's first year of operations, appropriates dollars into the fund equal to current federal spending on 1) Medicare, 2) Medicaid, 3) the Federal Employee Health Benefits Program, 4) Tricare, 5) "programs providing general hospital or medical assistance," and 6) "any other federal program identified by the Secretary."

For future years, appropriates dollars "equal to the amount appropriated to the Trust Fund for the previous year, adjusted for reductions in costs resulting from the implementation of this Act, changes in the consumer price index for all urban consumers for the fiscal year involved, and other factors determined appropriate by the Secretary." *The Senate bill does* not *include this provision.*

States that "any other provision of law in effect on the date of enactment…restricting the use of federal funds for any reproductive health service shall not apply" to dollars in the trust fund.

TITLE VIII—CONFORMING AMENDMENTS TO THE EMPLOYEE RETIREMENT INCOME SECURITY ACT (ERISA)

Section 801—Prohibition of Employee Benefits Duplicative of Benefits under the Medicare for All Program; Coordination in Case of Workers' Compensation

Amends ERISA to prohibit employer coverage of benefits covered by the new health program. Requires workers' compensation carriers liable for services furnished to reimburse the program for such services.

Section 802—Application of Continuation Coverage Requirements under ERISA and Certain Requirements Related to Group Health Plans

Amends ERISA to state that continuation coverage requirements only apply to employer health plans that do not duplicate payments for items or services covered under the new program. *The Senate bill would repeal this requirement entirely.*

Section 803—Effective Date

Makes the amendments effective on the effective date of the new program.

TITLE IX—ADDITIONAL CONFORMING AMENDMENTS

Section 901—Relationship to Existing Federal Health Programs

Sunsets benefits provided under Medicare, Medicaid, the Federal Employee Health Benefits Program, and Tricare two years after enactment (i.e., the effective date of the new program). States that school health programs and centers currently funded by Medicaid "shall be continued and covered" by the new program. Provides that "nothing in this act shall affect the eligibility of veterans" for services provided by the Department of Veterans Affairs, or of Indians for services provided by the Indian Health Service.

The Senate bill ends these programs when the new program takes effect, four years after the date of enactment. The Senate bill preserves the Medicaid program only to provide institutional long-term care services, and any services not covered by the new program. The Senate bill includes maintenance of effort provisions for states regarding these services, as outlined in Section 204 above.

Section 902—Sunset of Provisions Related to the State Exchanges

Ends provisions related to the state exchanges, and the subsidies provided through them, two years after enactment (i.e., the effective date of the new program). *The Senate bill would end these programs when the new program takes effect, four years after the date of enactment.*

Section 903—Sunset of Provisions Related to Pay-for-Performance Programs

Eliminates a series of provider pay-for-performance programs established under Obamacare and other laws two years after enactment (i.e., the effective date of the new program). *The Senate bill does not contain this section.*

TITLE X—TRANSITION

Section 1001—Medicare for All Transition

Amends the Social Security Act to allow individuals under age 18, over age 55, or currently enrolled in Medicare to enroll in the new program one year after enactment.

The Senate bill includes similar provisions, which allow individuals to purchase a plan consisting of Medicare Part A (hospital services), Part B (physician services), and Part D (prescription drug) benefits, or a Medicare Advantage plan. Eligibility would extend to individuals over age 55 as of January 1 the year after enactment, individuals over age 45 as of January 1 the second year after enactment, and individuals over age 35 as of January 1 the third year after enactment.

Premiums would consist of the average per beneficiary cost to provide benefits to eligible individuals (i.e., the buy-in population). Individuals will not be eligible for Medicare cost-sharing assistance, but would be eligible for Obamacare premium and cost-sharing subsidies, if they otherwise qualify (i.e., they meet income limits and do not have an offer of "affordable" employer coverage). The buy-in plan would also satisfy Obamacare's individual mandate.

Section 1002—Establishment of the Medicare Transition Buy-In

Requires the secretary to establish, effective one year after enactment and lasting through the effective date, a Medicare transition buy-in on the exchanges. The plan shall be available only on the exchanges, be open to "any United States resident," cover all the services available under the new program, and have an actuarial value (percentage of average health expenses covered by insurance) of 90%.

All participating providers in the current Medicare or Medicaid programs shall participate in the buy-in program, but will be reimbursed as provided for in the new program. The plan will have premiums that vary by family size, age, and tobacco status, as provided for under current federal law (i.e., Obamacare).

Makes the transition buy-in plan eligible for current (i.e., Obamacare) premium and cost-sharing subsidies, which will be available to all individuals regardless of income. (Current law limits eligibility to households with incomes between 100-400% of the federal poverty level, or up to $103,000 for a family of four in 2019.) Provides subsidies on a sliding scale, such that households with incomes more than 150% of poverty—$18,735 for an individual, and $38,625 for a family of four, in 2019—will pay no more than 5% of their income in premiums.

The Senate bill includes an additional Section 1011, which sets a maximum out-of-pocket spending limit for current Medicare beneficiaries of $1,500, effective on January 1 of the year following enactment. That spending limit would apply to all covered services under Medicare Part A (hospital coverage) and Part B (physician coverage). In addition, this section would eliminate the current Medicare Part A and Part B deductibles, beginning on January 1 of the year following enactment.

The Senate bill includes an additional Section 1012, which would reduce the maximum out-of-pocket spending limit for current Medicare beneficiaries' Part D drug costs to $305 per year. This change would take effect beginning on January 1 of *the year following enactment.*

The Senate bill includes an additional Section 1013, which would make dental services, vision services, and hearing aids and examinations for hearing aids covered services under the current Medicare program. These changes would take effect beginning on January 1 of the year following enactment.

Section 1011—Eliminating the 24-Month Waiting Period for Medicare Coverage for Individuals with Disabilities

Strikes current language that requires individuals who qualify for Social Security disability benefits to wait 24 months before becoming eligible for the current Medicare program. The changes take effect on December 1 after the date of enactment, and expire on the effective date for the new program.

The Senate bill includes this provision as Section 1014. The Senate bill also includes a Section 1015, which would prohibit issuers of Medigap supplemental insurance policies from denying the issuance of a policy, or discriminating in the pricing of that policy, "because of health status, claims experience, receipt of health care, or medical condition."

Section 1012—Ensuring Continuity of Care

Requires the secretary to keep all individuals, particularly those with disabilities or chronic conditions, from disruptions in care during the transition period, including in their provider teams. Prohibits employer plans and health insurers from ending coverage for enrollees "except as expressly agreed upon by the plan," or ending coverage or imposing conditions on individuals with disabilities or chronic conditions, "until all ages are eligible to enroll" in the new program. *The Senate bill includes similar provisions as Section 1021, except that the Senate bill does not explicitly prohibit employer plans and health insurers from ending coverage for individuals during the transition period.*

TITLE XI—MISCELLANEOUS

Section 1101—Definitions

Defines terms used in the bill: Group practice; Individual provider; Institutional provider; Medically necessary or appropriate; Provider; Secretary; State; and United States.

Section 1101 of the Senate bill would increase the asset limits for Supplemental Security Income (SSI) assistance. Under current law, individuals eligible for SSI cannot have outside resources of more than $2,000 for an individual and $3,000 for a couple. (The term "resources" excludes the value of a primary home, one car, personal household effects, life insurance policies, burial plots, and certain other assets.) The bill would raise these levels to $4,100 for an individual and $6,200 for a family, and index them to inflation in years after 2019.

The Senate bill includes its definitions as Section 1102.

Section 1102—Rule of Construction

Allows states to set additional standards or apply state or local laws, but only if they "provide equal or greater" eligibility and access to benefits, "do not reduce access to benefits," "allow for the effective exercise" of physicians' professional judgement, and remain consistent with the act.

Explicitly retains state licensure of health-care providers. Indicates that the act shall not diminish employers' or employees' rights under existing law or collective bargaining agreements. Indicates that states may not prohibit providers from participating in the program "for reasons other than the ability" of that entity to provide services.

The Senate bill does not include this section, but includes similar provisions in Section 206 of the bill.

Chris Jacobs, the Founder and CEO of Juniper Research Group, has spent more than 15 years studying health care on and off Capitol Hill. He has analyzed health policy and legislation for some of the leading lights of the conservative movement—including Jim DeMint, Bobby Jindal, Mike Pence, Pat Toomey, and Jeb Hensarling. While working for the House Republican Conference under then-Chairman Mike Pence, he helped lead the messaging against Obamacare in the run up to the law's passage. After the law's enactment, he continued his work for the Senate Republican Policy Committee, Joint Economic Committee, and Heritage Foundation. Chris serves as a Senior Contributor to *The Federalist*, and previously contributed to the *Wall Street Journal's Think Tank* blog. He has taught classes on health care policy for the Conservative Policy Institute, and at The American University, from which he graduated Phi Beta Kappa with a degree in Political Science and History.